CHANGE AGILITY

A GUIDE TO HELP YOU THINK ABOUT CHANGE
MANAGEMENT DIFFERENTLY

JASON LITTLE

CONTENTS

PART III - MY TAKE - MODERN CHANGE MANAGEMENT PRINCIPLES

PART IV - CHANGING YOUR VIEW OF CHANGE

PART V - WHAT'S CHANGE SINCE LEAN CHANGE MANAGEMENT?

CHASING CARS (WHY THIS BOOK? WHY NOW?)

"The way forward is paradoxically not to look ahead, but to stop and look around" - John Seely Brown

* * *

In 1974, Southwest Airlines was in its infancy and on the verge of collapse. They needed to sell one of their four planes, but still had to service a four-plane schedule. The best way to do this was to get people off and on the plane as fast as possible.

Thus, the 10-minute turnaround was born.

At the time, there were fewer constraints on air travel than today. Passengers would be waiting on the tarmac to get on the plane, and people would still be finding their seats while the plane was pushing back from the gate.

To save their airline back then, Southwest had to understand their constraints and everything involved with deplaning, prepping, and boarding flights without much outside help. They had to create it from scratch.

Today, information is largely free and easy to obtain. If we need to create a continuous improvement program, develop a multi-team agile process, or transform our organization, Google can do most of the work for us.

Then we create some slides, strategic pillars, and other stuff to make stakeholders feel confident that we're headed in the right direction, even though no one knows exactly how to do this.

Creating a change framework is reasonably simple. There are certain universal ideas that are relevant in any context. That's why so many of the frameworks you can find with Google has assessment, analysis, execute, and close out phases. The Shewhart Cycle, often attributed to Deming, of Plan-Do-Check-Act is the only model we need, but as you know, the devils are in the details.

Changing today's organizations is harder than it's ever been. We're bombarded daily with new models, frameworks and tools that promise to ensure successful change, and make us feel good about an unknown and unknowable future. When these models, frameworks, and tools don't live up to their promises after 12-18 months, the VP of Transformation is out on their ass and a different consulting firm tags in with their All Purpose Method based on the latest neuroscience findings.

Back in 2007, the trainer who taught me Scrum told many stories of helping a large financial institution, transform to agile, and here we are 12 years later, and they're still transforming.

Somewhere along the way, we've confused the natural evolution all organizations continually go through with one-trick pony transformation schemes, and it's frustrating the hell out of everyone.

WHY THIS BOOK, WHY NOW?

Jerry Weinberg[1] influences much of my work and train of thought. I remember when asked about his most significant contribution to software he replied, "I never invented another programming language."

That's the intent of this book.

For more than 15 years, I've helped many organizations, teams, and people adopt agile practices in software, HR, change management, organizational development, marketing and more.

I wanted to use their stories, journals, and pictures to show three main views of looking at *agile change management:*

- Transforming how you manage change work.
- Transforming how you think about change.
- Transforming how you work with agile teams.

Agile change frameworks, methods, playbooks, and processes can be valuable, but they are based on someone's view and experiences of how they think you should do it.

This book revisits the intent of agile to make you think about why you want to do agile change management. That will allow you to create a unique approach to match your context versus trying to plug in someone else's square peg into your context's round hole.

In the words of Jerry Weinberg, a little jiggle can go a long way, and I hope the stories in this book inspire you. What's different about this book is that this static artifact is just the beginning. In true agile fashion, it'll live on and evolve via change-wayfinder.com[2]

While it's understandable that we want change to have a start, middle, and end, it never has and will never work that way. It's more like a wave caused by the push-and-pull of the organizational tides.

You need to find the right way to intervene in the organizational system, at the right time, to take one step forward.

As James Carse[3] said before Simon Sinek re-purposed his ideas[4], all organizations are playing an infinite game, not a finite one.

YOUR AGILE ISN'T MY AGILE

*We want answers; we want them now! Ask Google "what is
<whatever>" and you'll get a snippet from some website that tells you
what it is.*

* * *

$\mathcal{I}$t's January 23, 2020, and I'm sitting in Helsinki,
Finland putting the finishing touches on this book at
the tail-end of a trip where I ran a couple of change workshops
with friend and colleague Andrew Annett.

For fun, I googled "what is agile," here's what I found:

*"Agile is a time-boxed, iterative approach to software delivery that
builds software incrementally from the start of the project, instead of
trying to deliver it all at once near the end."*

Today, after finding this book on an old backup drive in August 2020, I googled it again and here's what Google's suggested answer was:

"Agile software development refers to a group of software development methodologies based on iterative development, where requirements and solutions evolve through collaboration between self-organizing cross-functional teams. ... Read more about the Agile Manifesto."

Both are process-focused, but the second one at least mentions the manifesto, so that's good!

I suppose that could be *good enough*, but what if I'm in marketing? Here is Google's answer to "what is agile marketing?"

"At its core, Agile marketing is a tactical marketing approach in which teams identify and focus their collective efforts on high value projects, complete those projects cooperatively, measure their impact, and then continuously and incrementally improve the results over time."

A little vague, but ok, I guess. How about for HR? Here's google's suggested answer for "what is agile HR?"

"Retros can also be held with hiring managers, particularly after a new 'HR event' like a hiring, firing, or performance review cycle. This is a 'customer-centric' approach that agile espouses. The point is to understand whether the work HR is doing is delivering the intended value."

If you're an HR person, please forget you read that. It's not anywhere *near* being related to agile's values and principles. It looks more like an opinion from someone familiar with Google's content ranking algorithm.

OK, I've got to try one more. Suppose I'm a software tester. Here is Google's answer for "what is agile testing?"

"Testing is a software testing process that follows the principles of agile software development. Agile testing aligns with iterative development methodology in which requirements develop gradually from customers and testing teams. The development is aligned with customer requirements."

Yikes, another dumpster fire, but I guess we can't fault Google for this. There are so many diverging opinions about what agile is nowadays; even the robots are confused.

We've reached a point where some organizations aren't *doing agile* anymore; they're doing *new ways of working* because there's too much baggage with the word 'agile':

"We called it a manifesto because it was a call to action based on our beliefs" - Martin Fowler

The History of the Agile Manifesto

Before you gloss over the rest of this chapter, thinking, *"Yeah, yeah, yeah...agile manifesto....I get it already"*, take a moment to pause and explore the idea. Re-read it, make a note of what's different now compared to when you first discovered it.

ᴇ agile manifesto was drafted in 2001 at Snowbird in Salt Lake City, Utah. Seventeen creators of various light-weight methods got together and created it because they wanted to uncover a better way of building software.

They agreed on the four values, had most of the 12 principles done during the workshop, and then refined them into what you can read today at http://agilemanifesto.org

> *Individuals and Interactions over Processes and Tools*
> *Working Software over Comprehensive Documentation*
> *Customer Collaboration over Contract Negotiation*
> *Response to Change over Following a Plan*

I've been using agile practises since the early 2000s, and have been helping organizations move towards *agile ways of working* since the mid-2000s. The word *agile* immediately fills people with preconceived notions of collaboration, building software faster/better/cheaper, and continuous improvement. Many people miss a few critical points:

1. The manifesto says, "While there is value on the statements on the right, we value the statements on the left more." We don't ignore documentation or planning; we value a tangible, working solution, and adaptation more.
2. The 12 principles derived from the values are often ignored. If you want to see how, simply google "business agility". Many, including me, wrote about this

a decade before the term was trademarked because we read the 5th principle.

3. Context matters. If you abstract away the software focus, you'll realize what the authors were saying is universally adaptable. It's precisely how Southwest approached their problems in 1974, and how Henry Ford approached revolutionizing car manufacturing in the early 1900s. Toyota deservedly gets the credit for what they did, but we all know Henry Ford was doing it first. Well, before Henry Ford, it was Oldsmobile that created the assembly line. Before that, I'm sure some folks were mass-producing something so *who invented it* doesn't matter.

4. Great organizations have chefs that continually evolve how they do the work while they do the work. That's the empirical nature of agile, and it's timeless: *learn to think in your context, and you'll be fine.*

There is much more to say about misconceptions of agile, but for now, let's go back to the intent of the agile manifesto and figure out how we can adapt that to change.

I promise you, if you start from the values and principles, and are congruent with how you derive your practices from them, you'll will unlock the power of agile.

HOW TO READ THIS BOOK

*a*ssuming you read the first two chapters, let me be *anti-agile* and tell you how I intend the rest of the book to be read. There are four main parts to this book:

1. The first part is an exercise for you to think about how you would adapt the agile manifesto to change. We often want to make *<insert discipline name here>* more agile, apply the practice, but we forget the values and principles it was based on. Esther Derby[1] once said, *"We apply the practice, but divorce the principle."*

2. The second part digs deeper into the principles. This is important, and often overlooked. People look at the four values and stop there, missing out on the fantastic principles. I'll remind you with a few questions to get you to reframe each principle from a software focus to a change focus.

3. The third part is where I'll share my view based on

coming from the agile world. Since the year 2000 I've worked as a product owner, Scrum master, team member, internal/external coach, trainer and consultant, and the values and principles have shaped my approach to change versus what I've seen with many change managers who pick a method or framework without considering their context.

4. The fourth part contains my views on the three points from the opening chapter: transforming how you management change work, transforming how you think about change, and transforming how you integrate with agile teams.

5. The fifth part contains details about what has changed at The Commission, the company the store in Lean Change Management is based on, and what has changed about how I view change after having spent the last 6 - 7 years traveling the world, training, and working in various organizations.

6. Parts VI and VII are random bits of information to point you to online resources, and to thank all of the wonderful people I've met and interacted with over the years.

You're more than welcome to skip the workbook part, but I hope you don't. There is plenty of false information about how to apply agile practices in a non-software context.

Many people talking about how to do agile in change have learned about agile in the late-adopter phase. That is, those who learned agile post-2014 were most likely introduced to it in large enterprises through big frameworks and process thinking.

They see agile as a way to do change *at people* harder and faster by using better processes. It's not their fault, it's the nature of ideas. Once they're out in the world, they're open to being twisted in many directions.

I wrote this book for those who want to pause and take time to understand the intent of agile and to return to a place of values and principles that guide how we act as change agents.

Here's an example of what to expect.

A STORY: THE TALE OF TWO MINDSETS

Many years ago, I was invited to speak at a traditional change conference. The moderator opened the conference with how they were going to do something *agile and innovative* called an Open Space[2] to kick things off.

They created four breakout areas, with pre-determined topics, each with a moderator who directed the conversation. The attendees sat in a semi-circle with the moderator in the middle. The moderator asked a question, someone answered it, and the moderator re-framed it and directed the next question.

That wasn't innovative, wasn't agile, and not even remotely close to what an Open Space is.

Had this been an agile event, it would have been a proper Open Space. There'd have been a pile of sharpies and paper in the middle of the room. The moderator would have described the rules of Open Space, and the entire day would have emerged based on what people wanted to talk about versus what the moderator wanted people to discuss.

How could two different communities use the same practice in completely different ways?

Easy.

Both see the world through a different set of lenses based on their values and guiding principles. The former values control and structure, while the latter values collaboration and trust.

What's worse, after that traditional change conference, there's an army of people now thinking that an Open Space is something that it absolutely is not.

WHY IT MATTERS

In the book, *The New Kingmakers*[3], Stephen O'Grady describes this in terms of how developers imprint on their first programming language. It shapes their view of programming, which is why you find so many one-trick pony developers who say they have twenty years of experience, but it's the same one year of experience repeated over twenty years. They'll compare all new languages to their first true love, and nothing will convince them that another language could be better.

This is true for all humans. We fall in love with the first *new thing* that aligns with our beliefs, and we compare everything to it.

This phenomenon is called imprinting[4], or baby duck syndrome[5]. So remember, when you see that agile change expert showing you a Gantt chart and referring to it as a Kanban board, don't walk...run away!

DERIVING PRACTICES FROM PRINCIPLES

While Open Space pre-dates the Agile Manifesto by a couple of decades, the 11th agile principle is a strong foundation for it:

The best architectures, requirements, and design emerge from self-organizing teams.

That makes sense for software, but what about the story of the command and control Open Space? Let's adapt that principle to suit the story:

The best learning experience emerges from self-organizing groups of people inspired by a topic.

What prevented the earlier conference organizers from using Open Space as intended? Was it a:

- **Competence problem**? Maybe no one on the organizing committee has been to a proper Open Space and didn't know how they worked?
- **Mindset problem**? Was the most dominant personality on the planning team the one who would get blamed if people had a bad experience?
- **Values problem**? Were the organizers behaving incongruently?

- **Principles problem**? Were there no building principles to operate from?
- **Customer problem**? Did they have preconceived notions about their audience? Maybe they thought the attendees would blame them for a bad experience if there wasn't enough structure.

There are plenty of reasons that could have led to the decision to run the Open Space the way they did.

All I know is that after having organized plenty of conferences and Open Spaces, someone always asks, *"What happens if no one has anything to talk about?"*

You may have read that and thought *"What's the harm?"*

Well, these hundreds of people are relying on experts to show them a practice designed for provoking meaningful dialogue. Yet, what they learned was a different way to control the narrative that coerced people into talking about what the organizers thought they should be talking about.

They're going to go back into their organizations and use a practice in the wrong way, and then wonder why it didn't work.

HOW I DESIGNED THE READING EXPERIENCE OF THIS BOOK

I designed this book to make you think, not give you another agile change framework or playbook:

- To show you the agile manifesto, so you are familiar with what it is and how it came to be.
- To have you create a change manifesto by adapting the agile manifesto's values and principles to change.
- To test what you created on a scenario.
- To share what I believe *agile change management* is all about, along with stories and examples of how I use the agile manifesto to guide my actions.

I'll go through each value and principle and give you short exercises to discover how to make the most of what already exists without creating a new framework or tossing out whatever framework you're using today.

After that, I'll give you a bunch of lean startup, agile, and design thinking practises and ideas that I've used, complete with pictures and stories, so you can see how these ideas have been used in real organizations. You can find more at the Change Wayfinder[6].

Finally, along the way you'll find URLs to visit where you can connect with other readers to see what they've done, so your peers can inspire you.

My goal is to help you see more options for nudging change forward by looking at change through different lenses. Once you have more choice and are more intentional about designing the right organizational intervention, the work will be more satisfying, the people will be happier, and the world will be a better place.

BEING AGILE OR DOING AGILE?

"We want to use agile on this project, but we don't want agile to get in the way."

* * *

*I*t feels like a lifetime ago, but I'll never forget my answer to that seemingly odd question from one of my clients, PMO Director, Jack, and Senior Manager of Development, Sally, *"Well, there are only four values, which ones should I ignore?"*

That same year, Sidney Crosby was hoisting his first Stanley Cup, Avatar was on its way to become the highest-grossing movie of all time, and Apple's flagship phone was the 3GS.

Jack and Sally were the head honchos of a thousand-person department in an 80,000 person organization that I'll call Big Co, that wanted to adopt agile across their department. Actually,

THEY didn't want to, someone else did. Looking back now, I don't even remember why this change came to be. Today, however, *every* organization wants to be more agile due to corporate peer pressure, but back then, who knows.

I had two main priorities at Big Co.

- The first was to train everyone on *doing* agile. That's right, everyone from developers to testers, to business people and-corporate trainers, to-executives and managers.
- The other was working as a Scrum Master on pilot teams. I worked with over 20 teams, including a non-software team that wanted to use agile for working on enterprise business process initiatives, so it's safe to say this experience was an incredible learning experience for me.

In addition to me, our coaching team at Big Co consisted of a senior agile coach and an Extreme Programming (XP) coach.

Fun Fact: The XP coach was directly responsible for me attending AYE that same year, which influenced the path I took. He told me I *"should"* go, and I *"should go to the sessions that made me feel uncomfortable"*. Had I not met Jerry Weinberg, Esther Derby, Johanna Rothman, Steve Smith, and Don Gray, the hosts of AYE, you wouldn't be reading this, and I'd probably still be working as a Product Owner somewhere. You can decide if that's good thing or not!

Our approach then was more or less the same as what I still see many organizations doing today:

- Train everyone (general agile, the methods we decided they will use etc.)
- Run pilot programs.
- Implement an agile software management tool.
- Rollout and scale.
- Push water uphill with a stick. (OK, I'm kidding with this one, but still.)

AGILE ADOPTION VS AGILE TRANSFORMATION

Back then, this approach was labelled *adopting agile.* People started calling themselves agile coaches, even though it wasn't a recognized job title in any organization I knew of. My official title was Agile Consultant, and I still distinctly remember being ostracized in agile circles for saying that we were simply consultants who specialized in agile stuff.

The argument against my belief was that there was something more noble and honourable about being an agile coach than a consultant.

Back then, the agile coach would roam the organization, free from the constraints of the hierarchy.–Today we have Agile Centres of Excellence (COEs) with seven layers of hierarchy:

- Junior Agile Coach
- Agile Coach I
- Agile Coach II

- Senior Agile Coach I
- Senior Agile Coach II
- Agile Program Director
- VP of Agile

Agile Transformation wasn't yet a thing, because the agile community, myself included, was clueless about organizational change. Agile was seen as an IT-only thing even though some small circles of people knew it wasn't. The problem was, outside of screaming, "AGILE AFFECTS THE WHOLE ORGANIZA-TION!!!" the agile community couldn't articulate what that meant.

At the time, The Agile Coaching Institute[1] was still a year away from existing, and none of the agile frameworks that dominate today's market existed. Scrum became the most popular agile approach because it was the most popular training course and certification that existed at the time.

While the term *agile coach* was in its infancy, Extreme Programming (XP) introduced the role of coach[2] in the '90s. The XP coach's responsibility was to help teams live the agile manifesto. While the technical bits were forefront, the focus was always on the first agile principle: Satisfy the customer through early and continuous delivery of valuable software.

Outside of the professional coaching world, I can't find any earlier reference to the term coach in a software context.

COMMON SENSE AGILITY

A few years before I started working at Big Co, I discovered big *A* agile by accident.

While working in my second startup, we used daily stand-ups (Scrum) and retrospectives (Scrum), limiting our work in progress to one big project, and two small projects concurrently (Kanban).

Oddly enough, it was through my dad, who worked as a boiler-maker for 30 years. They used plenty of agile practices during a time when the Broad Street Bullies were dominating hockey. You can even see it at a Walmart if you go early enough in the day. They do *enterprise daily stand-ups*, as do many retailers, restaurants and more non-IT businesses.

Our team at Big Co was responsible for new development, media catalogue management, and support and maintenance, so the way we worked, *worked* for us. As our company grew from 3 to 30, then to 200, we adapted our processes from the team up, not the other way around.

It felt natural; it was collaborative and straightforward, so once I joined Big Co, I made the mistake of thinking that organic change could work too. I still remember Jack's office's exact location, where I had that initial conversation that felt more like a pre-emptive strike on his part.

It would be a couple of years before I'd understand what Jack and Sally were saying:

If the project goes to hell, it's our ass, not yours, or the team's.

The next decade-and-a-bit would see the rise and fall of various agile movements like the agile readiness assessment phase, the 'doing vs being' debates, the enterprise framework phase, and the certification pyramid scheme phase.

Now I'd say we're in the *<agile + function> phase*, which defeats the purpose. If all of our functional departments are 100% agile, we've optimized the parts, not the whole.

This is the fundamental difference in how agile people see agile versus how traditional change people see agile.

Agile people have been unknowingly doing organizational change work and have been looking to understand how to make sense of what they see. Traditional change people have been applying change methods and frameworks and now want to apply agile change methods and frameworks.

One is people-centric, the other only pretends to be.

One is problem-focused, the other is solution-to-an-unknown-problem-focused.

Let me be clear about those last points.

We are all doing the best we can with what we have[3] based on who we are and how our experiences have shaped how we see the world.

Just because someone takes notes at a daily standup to satisfy governance, it doesn't make them an idiot. I believe most change agents' intent, whether it's agile coaches, change people, HR folks, and more, is good. Sometimes it manifests itself in appearing like a know-it-all fixer, but the intent is always to be helpful.

Great change agents flip the bit from *me* to *we* so hopefully this book gives you ideas and a few different lenses to help you do that.

BECOMING MORE FULLY HUMAN

*H*ow we behave as change agents stems from who we are as a person. That includes how we grew up, where we grew up, what period we grew up in, and all the personal and professional experiences we've had.

In his fantastic book, *The Organized Mind*[1], Daniel Levitin describes how every generation has their complaints.

- When people invented writing to track inventory, some thought the lack of storing things in our brains would make us stupid.
- When TV was invented, the previous generation who grew up without it thought it would make their kids stupid.
- When tablets were invented, parents who grew up without it thought it would make their kids stupid.

I'm sure when AI, VR and having chips embedded in our heads becomes the norm, that generation will say something similar, "Back in my day, we didn't a computer chip to tell us what to do...we just googled it" ~need

In Levitin's view, humans are lazy, and we create technology to offload activities from our brain to focus on more complex problems.

The older I get, the more relaxed and pragmatic I get. I think.

I remember my first agile coaching gig where they were going to implement agile the "right way", no matter the context.

I'm sure the idea of this book or the structure of it will confuse some people. Here's the best way I can summarize why I've organized it this way:

- We live in a quick-fix, not-invented-here society. Everything you need to be more agile is contained in the manifesto if you can translate it from a software to non-software context.
- How you use the practices you use is determined by the principles you live by, not the principles of its creators.
- Those principles are influenced by a core set of values. Your values are different from mine, which are different from the creators of the practices you're using.
- Those values have emerged from the core of who you are.
- The core of who you are is shaped by your upbringing.
- The core of who you are is continually reinforced by your experiences.

But, and this is big:

You can consciously choose to change if you're willing to work at it.

Remember the story in Chapter 3: How to Read This Book? The organizers of that conference were smart, capable people who didn't get to enjoy the freedom and power of a proper Open Space.

Had someone been able to convince the rest of the organizers to give it a shot, and do a true Open Space, who knows how that would have influenced the people.

In Lean Change Management, I referenced the basics of the Satir change model. Here, I'll briefly introduce you to three other pieces of the Satir landscape[2]:

1. Coping stances
2. The five freedoms
3. Seven A's: stages for growth and actualization

COPING STANCES

At the heart of the Satir landscape and all interaction are ourselves, others, and the context. *Others* may include a partner, co-worker, or group of people. The *context* is the situation or container of the interaction between us and others.

Placating: When we ignore ourselves and turn the stress of the context inwards. "Oh, I'm sorry, it's my fault, I'll do whatever you need."

Blaming: When we ignore the other the turn the stress of the context outwards. "You idiot, you screwed this up, it's your fault."

Irrelevant: When we ignore the context and deflect the stress of the context. [In response to your co-worker getting fired] "Well, I guess you won't have to get up early anymore!"

Super-reasonable: When we ignore ourselves and others and consider only the context. "It doesn't matter what either of us think, the change has to get done."

Congruence: When we consider ourselves, others and context. "I'm sad that you got fired, but I am not able to process this now so is it ok if I call you tomorrow?

FIVE FREEDOMS

1. The freedom to see and hear what is here, instead of what "should" be, was, or will be.
2. The freedom to say what you feel and think, instead of what you "should" feel and think.
3. The freedom to feel what you feel, instead of what you "ought" to feel.
4. The freedom to ask for what you want, instead of always waiting for permission.
5. The freedom to take risks on your own behalf instead of choosing to be only "secure."

I learned from Jerry Weinberg, at AYE that the way things are, are not the way they need to be.

SEVEN A'S

The seven As are grouped into three buckets representing our internal process for change, interacting with others, and finally embedding the change into who we are.

Peace: The peace within the individual

1. **Awareness**: Becoming aware of the desire to change. That might mean changing out of necessity (my company went bankrupt and I'm out of a job in a month) or changing out of unhappiness with the status quo (I don't like my job, I want to change careers.)

2. **Acceptance**: Not acceptance of the change, but acceptance of who we are. Accept yourself for who you are, then meaningful change can happen.

3. **Authorship**: Taking ownership and realizing you have more choice than you may have thought initially.

Peace: The peace between partners in a relationship

4. **Articulation**: Communicating our intent that we want to change, and possibly asking for help from others.

5. **Application**: Practicing the new behaviours as a result of the change.

6. **Activism**: Becoming change agents that help people go through what we just went through.

Peace: The peace among the participants in a greater community.

⑦ **Altruism**: Becoming congruent (valuing ourselves, other people, within any context).

WHY THIS MATTERS TO ME

This is just a shallow–dip into the Satir landscape, which I believe is suitable for this book. I recommend visiting satirglobal.org to learn more. When we are aware of who we are, and accept it, we are more well-prepared to integrate with the world around us in a more human way.

Let's go back to the Open Space example.

It might appear that I'm blaming, that isn't my intention. Again, remember that this book intends to help you become congruent with how you behave when you say you want to be more agile in change management.

Suppose the lead organizer described Open Space and then said,: "None of us have tried this before, so we don't know what will happen. Our intention is to explore cutting edge topics that are important to you, so we're going to have a short retrospective afterwards to get your thoughts."

That may have changed everything.

BETA VERSION 1.0? WTF?

*H*ere we are in October 2020, and I'm doing the final proofing of this book. I released it as Beta 0.1 in August, got feedback, validation on the ideas, and then hired a proper copy-editor to help! Writing a book is undoubtedly a high effort, with questionable return.

Who knows if anyone will like the ideas, so instead of doing what I did with Lean Change Management (getting a producer, beta readers, focus groups, graphics people, copy editing, structure editing etc), I decided to write it, clean it up with Grammarly, and just release it.

This book poured out of me like a leaky bag of milk. (Yeah, in Canada we have bagged milk. Weird, eh?)

An entertainer I follow released a TV series this way. One day it just showed up with no fan-fair. I like this approach because with so much hype and anticipation, there's no way the product will live up to it, especially in today's world.

The funny thing is, there are a few missed typos in my first book and some people on Amazon feel the need to point that out. If you find a typo and THAT is your biggest complaint, well, that's fine with me.

I have a CD from a major artist from back in the day where the song order on the jacket doesn't match the actual order of the songs. That doesn't make me hate their music.

My point is, the return on finding a couple of typos, isn't worth the effort, especially with untested ideas, so I'll pull a Google and slap a beta on this book. Remember, it lives on via change-wayfinder.com!

NO RIGHT, WRONG, GOOD, BAD, SMART, OR STUPID!

You've already read a few stories, and there are plenty more in the remaining chapters.

I will tell stories where the change folks, or organizations did things that I thought didn't make sense. We live in a world obsessed with doing things right the first time.

Hell, even agile people will say, *"Experiment and fail fast!"* Yet these same people will chastise companies for not getting it right the first time!

I tell you these stories without pointing fingers, or shaming them for doing their own thing. That isn't my intent.

My intention is to help you find options that will allow you to find the right experiment for your context. Don't avoid disrupting the system because it'll be hard, but also don't disrupt the system just for the sake of disruption.

I believe everyone is doing the best they can with what they have, in the environment they find themselves in.

I also believe there are enough existing ideas that if we all stop and look around once in a while, we'll find the right inspiration to leave the world better than how we found it.

I hope this book inspires you.

PART I - MODERN CHANGE MANAGEMENT MANIFESTO

"We're going to sprint on an epic. Let's get you in and help the team"

* * *

Many years ago, I worked with a marketing team that wanted to adopt agile. I had worked with their IT teams a year earlier, and now pockets of non-software groups and divisions at this company wanted to use it.

The VP of Marketing and Digital wanted an agile coach to help a pilot team use agile practices to get stuff done more effectively. I had good relationships with marketing-while working with their IT teams, so it was an easy leap for me.

If you boil away the noise about *transforming to agile,* this is a typical organizational change, and it's essential to think of it that way.

- Why did they want *this* change? And why now?
- Why would people on the marketing teams care and want to work differently?
- What help and support would the people need. Would they actually want help to become more agile?
- How transparent should the transformation process be?
- What's the entry point into the team, and how do we get started?

No matter the change, there is always a certain amount of change readiness that needs to happen. But, it doesn't need to be a big production.

In this case, the leaders already decided to do the change, so my approach was simple:

- Design a liftoff for the entire stack (VPs, managers, and people on the pilot team).
- Have the VPs explain to the team about why this was important to them and the organization.
- Talk about the *epic* they were going to *sprint* on. (I'll explain what that means later!)
- Do some basic training, and team onboarding which I'll refer to as a *liftoff*.
- Create a coaching agreement for me and the team, so we all know what to expect, what the boundaries are, etc.

Before I continue, remember that I said that the leaders already *decided* to do the change. Many change agents fall into the *have-to* trap before they even get started. That is, they think they have to blindly execute the order given by the leaders.

While the leaders already decided to make marketing *go agile*, in this case, it's still my responsibility to unpack the problem to solve and guide them on how to go about it. Odds are, they want marketing programs to happen faster, so once the teams are aware of that, they probably have a simple solution that won't require a big transformation.

During the liftoff with marketing, we agreed on an uncomplicated process, no PowerPoints, face-to-face communication, short feedback loops, and working agreements between the people on the team.

A quick sidebar about the PowerPoint thing. During the liftoff, I joked, *"Oh, and it's not agile to create a 43-page PowerPoint with the results. I just need all of you -(I pointed at all the VPs) just come down to this room at the end of the week and we'll show you what we did in 30 minutes or less."* They agreed because they admitted they never read or liked the communicate-by-PowerPoint culture.

So, back to the marketing team's move to agile.

We started by exploring what agile meant to them in their context, which meant starting with the agile manifesto:

Individuals and interactions over processes and tools.
Working software over comprehensive documentation.
Customer collaboration over contract negotiation.
Responding to change over following a plan.

There are two ways we used this manifesto. First, I used it as a guide for building the liftoff. I considered the VPs, managers, and staff to be the product, and if I was going to develop that product in an agile way, how would I approach it?

Second, I gave the team the manifesto and had them decide what it meant to them terms of doing marketing work. How we worked would be derived from how the team viewed the manifesto in their context.

INTERNALIZING WHAT AGILE MEANS

"We're going to sprint on an epic" - the opening of this chapter sounds a little weird. *Epics* meant *projects* and *User Stories* meant tasks or *customer journey statements*. The marketing team used these terms because most of the team went to Scrum Master training and tried to match what they learned to their reality:

- Going to a sprint meant being assigned to a cross-functional marketing team that would apply Scrum
- Sprinting on an epic meant the one-week time period where they'd work on the project.
- Epic owner was the product owner

Here is the crucial part: While they were not using the correct terms, they were at least trying to fit them into their context. I wasn't going to nitpick the language.

Remember, the purpose of this book isn't to teach you Scrum, so if you want more details, check out this short video from Lyssa Adkins[1]

For our purposes, here's a basic overview of Scrum, let's assume:

- We have a cross-functional team with people who have all the skills needed to deliver the solution. That includes change managers if necessary.
- We are working on 1-week iterations
- We are working on a 1-month release cycle (yes the goal is to have a potentially shippable product at the end of each sprint, but let's assume there is an outside constraint we can't change right now)
- A Sprint planning session starts the week
- We do a 15-minute standup every day to co-ordinate
- We do a backlog refinement session half-way through the week to prepare stories for the next sprint
- We hold end of week sprint reviews and retrospectives

Here's how we adapted Scrum to the marketing team's reality:

- We had a cross-functional marketing team representing six marketing sub-departments
- We used 1-day long sprints.
- We used a weekly release cycle
- We started each day with a 30-minute planning session
- We did a daily standup at 1 pm every day
- We did a sprint review with the *Epic owner* at 2:30 every day, followed by a short retrospective
- We closed the day with a proper, team-only, retrospective and backlog refinement session to be ready for the next day

While we broke some of the rules of Scrum, the benefits were identical. We:

- **Didn't have handoffs** with downstream marketing groups since all groups were represented on the Scrum team
- **Received fast-feedback** from *Epic owners* even though they couldn't be with the team 100% of the time
- **Ran an empirical process** that evolved over time and from team to team
- **Relied on the team to self-organize**

THE OUTCOMES

- **Completed in one week** what usually took three months, according to the VP of Marketing. This wasn't magic; this was because of focus and the complete removal of handoffs.
- **It spawned seven other marketing team experiments**, all of which worked more or less the same way, except for one go-to-market sprint which failed miserably
- **A change to the overall marketing program process.** They created a highway analogy to better manage their process. If uncertainty was high, they used the HOV lane (also known as - *sprint on an Epic*). If uncertainty was low, for go-to-market initiatives for example, they stayed on the regular highway.

Essentially, for new epics they decided on which process to follow and learned that business as usual, or repeatable work, didn't benefit at all from this new process.

That's why I mentioned earlier that the go-to-market sprint failed miserably. The team knew precisely what to do, how long it would take, and how much it would cost. The effort to change that process was high, and it made execution worse.

Agile approaches work better when uncertainty is high. It doesn't mean it won't work for repeatable, predictable work, it means you'll have to make a choice. The effort to change for the sake of having a consistent process across teams might not be worth it.

MODERN CHANGE MANAGEMENT?

What's so modern about this? Sounds like good facilitation to me. Here's the difference:

In traditional change management you would:

- Create a stakeholder map, vision statement, resistance mitigation plan, etc.
- Do a change readiness assessment with the entire marketing department (~600 people)
- Assign a project manager to manage stuff
- Devise a playbook or standard process model in isolation that all teams will use
- Test on a few pilots

- Roll it out if it works, tweak it and roll it out if it didn't work
- Close the initiative down

In modern change management you would:

- Co-create a way forward with a facilitated conversation (the liftoff I did that involved everyone in the first experiment)
- Validate assumptions (take action sooner, include stakeholders at the end of each experiment, and use those learnings for the next experiments)
- Create an adaptable process driven by the teams (their highway analogy)
- Give teams freedom to create their own unique process within a set of reasonable constraints
- Have people who participated in the first experiments became advocates and 'trainers' for new teams

The fundamental difference is that the modern *gave the organization choice*. That's why I use it. Had I followed a static agile playbook with them, it would have been the wrong approach for them. By taking the stance of a coach, and problem solver supported by modern ideas, I gave them the choice about how to proceed.

I have seen this many times over the years. The consulting firm imposes their model on the organization and forgets about the context. Jerry Weinberg calls this *dropping the change through the hole in the floor*.[2]

The approach I use is more like his diffusion approach[3], which is more like adding milk to coffee. And no, Niels Plfaeging didn't invent that term[4], but I absolutely love his work!

HOW TO FLIP FROM TRADITIONAL TO MODERN

In the next chapter, I'll show you specially how I adapted the agile manifesto to this change, and how the team adapted the agile manifesto to their non-software context.

But first, I want you to create a change manifesto that captures the spirit of the agile manifesto. I've run this exercise in my workshops since 2014, and it's always interesting to see how people modify the agile manifesto from a software focus to a change focus.

Here's your task.

You've been assigned to create an agile change management process. Using the agile manifesto as a guide, how would you re-write it to suit a change management context?

Here's something to get you started. The agile manifesto says, *working software over comprehensive documentation.*

As change agents, we're not *delivering software* so how would you change that?

In the next chapter, I'll give you more detailed instructions if you're stuck. Check out what others have come up with at changeagility.org[5]. If you're brave enough, you can share your non-software manifesto there too.

YOUR CHANGE MANIFESTO

*H*opefully, you didn't jump to the chapter with some examples! I guess it doesn't matter if you did, but I always like to document my thoughts first, and then see what others think.

These are the instructions for the exercise I do in my workshop:

Given the four values of the agile manifesto, how would you write a change manifesto that captures the spirit of the agile manifesto for guiding how you approach change work?

For example, the second value of the agile manifesto is *Working Software over Comprehensive Documentation*. Suppose you're working on a re-organization and you're not delivering software. **How would you change that value to suit the context?**

The rules for this exercise are simple:

- You can have as many, or few, statements as you like. You don't have to have four just because the agile manifesto has four.
- If you want to "apply agile to change management" your manifesto should capture that somehow
- After you create your manifesto, I'll give you a little scenario to test it, along with a link where you can see what other people did in the same scenario.

THE HARD PART

It's time for you to do some work! You might be reading this book on a eReader, so grab a scrap of paper, or whiteboard, and think about it.

Compare your manifesto with others at changeagility.org[1]

ENACTED THEORY VS ESPOUSED THEORY

Today's business world is polluted with easy answers. I could write the statement, *"It doesn't matter how agile you are, the best organizations focus on outcomes,"* and some people would jump out of their seats screaming, *"YES!!! You're SOOO, right!!!"*

It's interesting, and you might believe it, but it's not useful.

Now that you have your change manifesto, here's your scenario:

The change you're working on isn't going well from the perspective of your executive sponsor. She sends you an email demanding you come up with a 12-month roadmap, including all specific activities and measurements you're going to use to ensure successful change.

You want to use an agile approach to this. Think about or write down what you'd do based on using your agile change manifesto as a guide.

INDIVIDUALS INTERACTING

Here's a short story about where the inspiration for this exercise came. A government organization was embarking on a multi-year change that would ultimately affect 8,000 people. The program lead, Jimmy, had watched a talk I gave at a local change conference and wanted to try some of these agile ideas.

We met for a couple of hours, and the most straightforward thing he agreed on doing was putting up a big visible wall, invited stakeholders in front of it once a week instead of status reporting, and ran daily stand-ups with the core change team.

That's it—no big plan, 73-page PowerPoint, or otherwise. The emphasis was put on making interactions between people easier versus focusing on building a complex agile change management process. Here's the email he sent me over a year later:

to me ▾

GP Tue, Mar 27, 2018, 4:02 PM ☆ ↰ ⋮

Hi Jason,

The project is going pretty well!! Starting iteration 3 testing and we're on target to go-live June 1st. I'm positive things would not be in as good shape, or have gone as smoothly without the "Lean Change" principles and ideas you shared with us early on.

We actually got enthusiastic senior management support to delay system go-live by 6 weeks exclusively to address risks and change insights identified based on your premise that "the people who help make the change don't fight the change". Our SAP implementation partners think we're crazy spending so much time & effort on change management.

Love the Kanban Board!! I've lost count of how many problems we've solved; landmines and pot-holes we've avoided during our weekly the 30 minute retrospective meetings at the Kanban board.

Attached is a project update slide deck we presented to management a few weeks ago.

...

IT'S YOUR CHOICE

I've told this story in many organizations, and some have said, *"Well, that'll never work* here...we are a global enterprise...blah blah blah."

That makes about as much sense as saying, *"I tried playing hockey; hockey doesn't work."*

This approach worked for Jimmy because he was the catalyst that wanted it to work. He influenced others with his positive energy, and the skeptics came along for the ride. It wasn't mandated, he just knew it was better for this situation, so he took action.

Since 2014, I've visited many organizations in many industries in over 12 countries, and the pattern has always been the same: A passionate change agent who catalyzes the people around them to make these ideas work. Change agents who are looking for the next magic process or best practice rarely make it work, not because of them, but because the change they're working on isn't necessary.

I have never been a fan of the term *mindset* because I think it's used as a stick, meaning *"I have a growth mindset, but those idiots I work with have a fixed mindset, how do I change them?"*

Some will say what I describe in this book is all about the mindset of the change agent, but I want to avoid that language in favour of looking at change through different lenses.

Remember **you have a choice.** Stay true to who you are, and if you believe what is in your manifesto, it will inspire others to approach change differently.

Now that you've created your change manifesto, I'll show you the two ways we used the agile manifesto to guide how I approached the change with the marketing team, and how they used it to approach their non-software work.

INDIVIDUALS AND INTERACTIONS

While there is value in the statements on the right, we value the statements on the left more.

* * *

$\mathcal{M}$any seem to skip past that footnote[1] on the agile manifesto and immediately leap to conclusions that agile is anti-process or anti-tool.

Agile could care less; it's agile practitioners that make this assumption based on *their* beliefs. That's why you see such divergence and conflict between agile camps. The Kanban people have their style, the Scrum people have theirs, and pragmatists mostly ignore the noise and do whatever works.

We all think we're pragmatists, but we're not. I was a Scrum zealot for years; then I accepted that I was being hired to help people solve problems versus installing methods.

HOW I CHANGED MY APPROACH TO CHANGE

I mentioned Jerry Weinberg's hole-in-the-floor approach in a previous chapter. The people at the top decide on the change and metaphorically drop it through the hole in the floor on top of the organization. It's then left to the change people to ensure successful change.

With this marketing team, the people at the top decided they wanted their people to work in a more agile way, so I set constraints based on using the first value of agile, *individuals and interactions over processes and tools.*

The norm would be for me, the change agent, to go away and create a plan, get sign off and buy-in, then go into execution mode.

Instead, I eliminated that waste by setting the constraint that the entire department needed to be involved in the liftoff. I didn't NOT have a process; I had an abstracted, meta-process, that was simple and good enough to co-create the change with everyone affected.

By doing this together, we discussed important topics like:

- What does the team expect from the coach?
- What does the coach expect from the team?
- What would success look like?
- How will we know if we're headed in the right direction?
- What aren't we going to change?
- What are our working agreements?

Since we had everyone in the liftoff, the interactions between us helped team members see what was important to me, the coach, and the sponsors, and vice-versa.

We built our approach together, made tradeoffs where we needed to and adapted when it made sense to do so.

HOW THE MARKETING TEAM CHANGED THEIR APPROACH TO NON-SOFTWARE WORK

Following this value was simple for the marketing team. We had representation from six marketing divisions, so we were able to solve cross-department challenges through our interactions.

Normally, one team would do their piece and pass it on to the next team. When we finished *sprinting on our epic,* the VP said what took us two weeks in the new process typically took three months due to handoffs and complicated processes.

While he made it sound like magic, all we did was get a cross-functional team together which dramatically reduced decision-making time.

The first agile principle is universal; when in doubt, get people together instead of creating another process or buying a tool.

ANOTHER SHORT STORY

I've worked in many enterprise organizations going through an agile transformation, and there is usually an Agile Centre of Excellence, an Organizational Change team, a Change Management team, a Process Improvement team, and sometimes two or three more departments with overlapping objectives.

When it comes to change, these teams end up competing with each other, leading to 700-page governance documents.

One large bank I worked with combined people from all of these groups to work from one purpose and vision. With people from different backgrounds and functional areas, they had different skills and knowledge, allowing for the best ideas to come to the surface quickly. This is when friction is a positive thing!

When tasked with change, here are some questions you can ask before starting the change:

- Who does this today?
- What is changing, and for who?
- What competing forces exist? (i.e. I worked with a team that was given an objective that was directly at odds with another team, so instead of just following orders, we challenged the assumptions around what we were being asked to do.)
- What possible unintended consequences exist?
- How formal are existing processes? What can we reuse? What processes need to be decommissioned?

The first value of the agile manifesto is designed to explore system boundaries, existing norms, and interactions between people, teams, and departments. Let's start exploring what exists today before we design new processes or force the use of new tools on people.

WORKING SOFTWARE?

"You fulfilled all the requirements, but that software doesn't solve my problem."

* * *

I've seen this so many times over the years. Teams get forced into fulfilling the order and they lose sight of the problem they've been asked to solve.

People know what software they need when they see it. The second agile value is about showing working software sooner, so you can adapt to the changing needs of the business or customers.

HOW I CHANGED MY APPROACH TO CHANGE

Following this value was similar to the last one. During the liftoff, we agreed to not use PowerPoint to document processes and communicate, which was the norm for them.

"Just send me the deck" was code for *"I don't have time for this conversation."*

We agreed on documenting **absolutely nothing** about the change process, and this worked because of the relationship and credibility I had from working there the last couple of years. I understood the feeling of safety in documenting this process, but it wasn't necessary. Yet.

HOW THE MARKETING TEAM CHANGED THEIR APPROACH TO NON-SOFTWARE WORK

It's easy for software projects. The team builds software; people use it and give feedback. If we're not delivering working software, how would we adopt this agile value?

During the liftoff, we explicitly discussed what our version of *working software* was:

- A market validation of the solution.
- An impact analysis of how to implement the solution.

Once we discussed the organizational boundaries and what the definition of done was, we were off to the races. This is where things get blurry. Any skilled, agile practitioner will immediately see that second bullet point and scream, *"HEY WAIT!!!! THAT'S NOT AGILE!!!!!" YOU SHOULD HAVE BUILT AND DEPLOYED THE SOLUTION!!! YOU CAN'T LOCALLY OPTI-MIZE LIKE THAT!!!"*

They would be right, but only in theory. As agile evolved over the last couple of decades, agile practitioners learned that there are substantial organizational forces at odds with agile delivery.

In this case, 25 teams needed to be involved in delivering our solution. It's easy to be an armchair change agent and say things like, *"We need to scale down our organizations"* or *"You really should be asking why they need 25 teams to do something so simple."*

Once agile exposes this problem to the organization, the organization can then choose to do something about it. If de-scaling is the answer, who decides who is let go? The agile coaches?

It's an over-simplification to say that we *could have just* built a complete cross-functional team to deliver the solution. We could have, but that would have involved 12 VPs coming together around a re-organization of thousands of people, which is a lot more work than was needed.

CUSTOMER COLLABORATION

"Let your handshake be a greater bond than any written contract." -
Steve Maraboli, Unapologetically You: Reflections on Life and the
Human Experience

* * *

C ontracts can be tricky. We put so much time and effort into creating them to combat inevitable what-if scenarios, and one of two things generally happens:

1. We never look at it again and just work together.
2. We use it as a stick to beat the other when the relationship goes sour.

More often than not, Scenario #2 is what happens.

Generally speaking, agile contracts are about fixed time and cost while scope becomes the variable.

For example, I was once sub-contracted by a consulting firm to be an agile coach for a 300-person organization.

After a week, there was no appetite from management to do anything, and I still had 30 days to fulfill. The CTO was very supportive, but he left the organization about a week after that making it even more difficult. I metaphorically roamed the countryside looking for problems that I could help solve.

Those included helping them merge their code repositories, automating release notes, visualizing the company history, and yelling at one douchebag of a team member who was just a complete asshole. None of which was what I was contracted to do.

HOW I CHANGED MY APPROACH TO CHANGE

As I mentioned, contracts are tricky, but necessary sometimes. I have a general base service agreement I use with organizations. It's general enough to say that my time and cost if fixed, the deliverables are up for negotiation. In one case, to get around an enterprise organizations incredible protection of OpEx (Operating Expense), we agreed to call what I was doing *project augmentation* instead of *agile coaching*.

Project augmentation activities could be billed to the department or project, while coaching and training would be considered OpEx. The latter would incite fear and riots across the organization since no one was allowed to increase OpEx without the blessing of the powers-that-be.

There were two main components that demonstrate how I lived this value:

1. Explicitly told the VPs that my scope is whatever it needs to be, and it'll vary from team to team. My cost and time will be fixed at "X billable hours per week", period.
2. Implemented a feedback measure by way of a modified Net Promotor Score (NPS) to determine if I lived up to the contract.

After each liftoff with the teams and the IT teams I previously worked with, I'd survey the team, which served as the feedback measure I mentioned, with these two main questions:

1. How likely would you recommend having a coach for teams that wanted to get started with agile?
2. How likely would you recommend the specific coach you had?

HOW THE MARKETING TEAM CHANGED THEIR APPROACH TO NON-SOFTWARE WORK

This is one of my favourite stories. While we were spinning our wheels on some assumptions, we realized we needed feedback from real customers.

Our epic owner knew the manager at the call centre and used $500 of her budget to give coupons to people who would stay on the phone to answer a couple of questions after calling support.

Within 24 hours, we received hundreds of pieces of feedback that helped us change our scope.

The lesson here: Contracts and agreements will always be necessary, but they shouldn't take the focus away from doing the right thing for the customer.

RESPONDING TO CHANGE

"Plans are worthless, but planning is everything."

* * *

*P*opular wisdom says Winston Churchill said this, but who knows. We have a history of incorrectly attributing quotes to the wrong person!.[1]

Adaptability is essential responding to events outside of our control. It doesn't mean that you *shouldn't* plan, and it doesn't mean that you're bad at planning.

It means that you've got to be aware of when to adapt to changing conditions, and especially those that you can't control. In today's world, organizations are less in control of their future than they used to be.

Remember the Southwest Airlines story? They adapted to the changing conditions of travel, and managed to do it without training their staff on agile practices. Looking at another giant, many focus on the demise of Kodak and it's failure to adapt to the shift to digital photography, but they're still around after 138 years. How'd they do that?

They focused on other areas of their business, like retro cameras, waterproof cameras and mobile accessories for taking photos with your phone[2]. While Kodak was slow to adapt and couldn't fight off the digital camera predators, they continued to make money selling and licensing their patents for technology, and have even expanded into new areas like blockchain technology and digital rights management.

The lesson in this story is: Don't parrot what you hear because it aligns with your beliefs, go read the story for yourself.

HOW I CHANGED MY APPROACH TO CHANGE

In Bigco's marketing department, I didn't change anything about how I approach change. I would say my approach changed in the late 2000s when I realized no organization was asking me to "make them agile" and train them on agile practices.

They were asking me to help them clarify a problem and to help them figure out options to move forward.

This value shaped my attitude as a change agent by teaching me how to make a "good enough" plan that was flexible enough to be adapted later.

HOW THE MARKETING TEAM CHANGED THEIR APPROACH TO NON-SOFTWARE WORK

In an earlier chapter, I wrote about how the go-to-market experiment failed miserably. I'm glad it did.

It was the second time we tried this sprint-on-an-epic process, and the backlash was so negative that the marketing department realized they couldn't have a standardized process that everyone must use.

That's why they created the highway analogy. The people that were part of the second experiment hated it and started bad-mouthing it to others, *"Oh, you don't want to get dragged to a sprint, they're awful."*

Instead of overcoming what we would typically label as resistance, we used that as input into adapting our plan.

There are debates in the agile community about the usefulness of the agile manifesto. Some say it's timeless; others say it's outdated, and some say it sucks just because seventeen white males created it.

I'm in the *it's timeless* camp. I believe that any group of people can be agile no matter what their context is. Remember my dad the boilermaker? He used agile practices in the '60s. Walmart uses them in retail today, and so do retail banks and other non-software businesses.

The key is, and this is stated in the agile manifesto, there is value in the statements on the right, and we value the statements on the left more.

In Part II, I'm going to switch over to the twelve agile principles and have you adapt those to change before showing you how I do it. Most of the myths with agile and continual invention of new methods came about because no one understood them, or worse, didn't even read them.

PART II - WORKBOOK - MODERN CHANGE MANAGEMENT PRINCIPLES

"Better to write for yourself and have no public, than to write for the public and have no self."— *Cyril Connolly, The New Statesman, February 25, 1933*

* * *

I'll never forget AYE in 2009 when Johanna Rothman ran a reinventing yourself workshop. I told her that I thought I wanted to do what she and the rest of the hosts did.

"Start writing", she said. So I did. I started a blog called *more agile than agile* because I fell into agile in a backwards way, plus I was a huge fan of Rob Zombie and loved the song More Human Than Human.

That lead to me writing *Lean Change Management* in 2013 because I thought it was an interesting story that people would want to hear. There was no intention to create workshops, online training, communities, or anything else.

Here we are today, and I've run hundreds of workshops in over 12 countries, and have enough content to write 5 books based on my experiences.

Writing the blog, and then the book, helped me find my style and refine my message. More importantly, it gave me an avenue to express my personal thoughts on the topic. Writing has always been a valuable endeavour for me because it's like therapy. It helps me make sense of my thoughts because sometimes I'm a mouth-thinker. We all have principles that we live by, and one of mine has been to help people find clarity or inspiration in something that prompts them to take action and make change happen for themselves.

So what exactly are *Modern Change Management Principles*? That sounds great in a tweet, but what the heck does it mean? How are *principles* different from *values*?

I've already shown you the Agile Manifesto values, so before I get into the principles, I'll define what I mean by the difference between values and principles.

Values are personal. They can change over time based on the experiences you have, and they'll evolve as you learn, grow, and age.

Principles are derived from values and are generally static. Principles don't change, but our situations do.

In my world, values shape your principles, which influence how you act. For example, if one of my values is *honesty*, my principles might be *I will not lie* and *I will not hide or withhold the truth.*

Those are two different things, and each will help us act in different scenarios. I won't outright lie, but I might be in a situation where withholding information could benefit me. That would be against my principles.

Subtle, but important.

I don't want to get too hung up on the strict definitions of values vs principles because our values, principles, and belief systems are symbolic and help shape who we are as humans.

The Agile Manifesto has four values and twelve principles. By themselves, the values don't provide enough information to help us take action. You could say that just looking at the values in isolation could have led to many of the agile myths we see today.

Have you heard someone in your organization say that *"we don't need to document stuff anymore because we're agile?"* Or, *"we don't need to plan; we can change things whenever we want because we're agile?"*

I have.

In *Part I - Modern Change Management Manifesto,* you created a change manifesto that captures the Agile Manifesto spirit. Then, you tested your manifesto on a scenario.

It might have been easy to know how to apply it without a set of principles designed to help you get to action, but imagine that your entire organization wants to live by the agile principles. It would be more difficult because each person's values will probably be different.

In the upcoming chapters, I'll show you how to adapt the twelve agile principles to change. More importantly, I'll help you understand how certain principles carry more weight depending on your environment and what kind of change your organization is going through.

This is where we start to move into the actionable ideas that unlock the power of using an agile approach in change management.

HOW PART II IS STRUCTURED

*E*ach of the following chapters will follow the same
pattern:

- I'll introduce the agile principle and share a short story
  about how the agile principle has guided me
- I'll ask you to rewrite the principle to fit into a change
  context by asking you questions about how you would
  change the principle from a software focus to a change
  focus.
- I'll close off with how I adapt it to a change context, and
  you can visit changeagility.org to see what others have
  come up with.

At the end of this Part, I'll share an exercise for how to co-create
your principles and prioritize them based on your organization's culture, type of change, and the composition of your
change team.

This is where things can get tricky! As defined in the previous chapter, principles are static, so why should they be different for an agile transformation or a multi-year software implementation that radically changes business processes?

Not every principle applies to each change in the same way. This is why I've mentioned that it isn't possible to have one all-encompassing change framework, method, or process. Much of the time, you're starting with universals that are generally true from change to change, but you adapt your approach based on the context.

Some of the principles you'll see in this chapter will be timeless and universal; others might need tweaking. Either way, this is a critical discussion to have during a liftoff with your change team or the people in your organization to establish the proper expectations.

This is the most difficult part of talking about principles. They will all sound good, but why does each agile organization behave differently if they're operating from the same values and principles?

That's the million dollar question, isn't it?

MIND THE PEOPLE

Our highest priority is to satisfy the customer through early and continuous delivery of valuable software.

* * *

*A*gile **Value**: Working Software over Comprehensive Documentation

While working as a product owner when tablets were first coming out, I was tasked with creating a new product. This was when the first iPad was coming to market so that'll tell you how long ago it was.

Since tablets were brand new, we figured they'd be popular, but had no idea what a tablet product could look like. Back then, responsive web design wasn't a thing, so our first idea was a microsite for investor relations (IR) clients. Instead of navigating big websites to find valuable IR information, these mobile applications would be like a quick reference guide and a showcase for IR clients.

So, there was no well thought-out strategy, only a gut feeling that tablets were going to be huge, and we wanted to be prepared.

We didn't know what *valuable software* was for these clients, so this principle morphed into:

My highest priority is to satisfy the customer through early and continuous validation of what's valuable to them.

ADAPTING THE 1ST PRINCIPLE TO CHANGE

Starting with this chapter, I'll ask you questions that will guide you through each agile principle and how you would adapt each statement to a change context.

1. What's our highest priority as change agents?
2. How do we fulfil that priority?
3. What's the change equivalent of "valuable software?"
4. What would *early and continuous* mean in a change context?

You are more than welcome to continue reading if you're in exploration mode, but if you'd like, re-write this principle from the perspective of being a change agent before you move on.

In Part III, I will share how I answered these questions. If you're impatient to see what others have done, you can connect with other change agents around the world via changeagility.org to see what they've done.

WELCOME CHANGE

Welcome changing requirements, even late in development. Agile processes harness change for the customer's competitive advantage.

✶ ✶ ✶

𝒜 **gile Value**: Responding to Change over Following a Plan

Remember the story from the *Customer Collaboration* chapter about the CTO who left and nobody else had interest in making things better? The CEO had said he wanted, *"150% effort, hands-on keyboards at all times...push..push..push"* at our first weekly update meeting.

I had 30 days of work left to do there so while I included this story to correlate to the *Customer Collaboration over Contract Negotiation* chapter, it fits here.

I *could* have renegotiated the contract to refine the scope, but instead, I bounced from team to team, helping them prioritize the most important things they needed help doing. I worked in week-long change sprints which gave me enough structure to live out those last few weeks.

The company was acquired a couple of months after my contract was up. I had always suspected that there was more going on than I knew about and this confirmed it.

ADAPTING THE 2ND PRINCIPLE TO CHANGE

Using these questions as a guide, how would you adapt the second agile principle to change?

1. What are the *changing requirements*?
2. Is *late in development* the *last responsible moment,* or irresponsible?
3. What about our change process prevents course correction?
4. What could change about how we do change that would make us more adaptable?

SHORT FEEDBACK LOOPS

Deliver working software frequently, from a couple of weeks to a couple of months, with a preference to the shorter timescale.

* * *

gile Value: Working Software over Comprehensive Documentation

I've worked in a few organizations where agile teams have extended the length of their sprints because it was too hard to get stuff done in a short time box.

Today, a *couple of weeks to a couple of months* can mean two weeks or an entire quarter. Still, this principle's core idea expands on the 1st Principle by being more specific about the "early and continuous" part.

I worked with a 300-person organization with five teams who were struggling to get all the work done in a two-week sprint.

Using this principle as a guide, we decided to try one-week sprints. It would force the team into breaking work down into smaller, more manageable pieces.

The teams admitted they hated that at the start. It was excruciating for them, but they agreed to try it for at least three sprints.

Eventually, they decided that one-week sprints were better than two-week ones, even if one-week sprints were more painful. They had a feeling once they expanded the time-box, they'd be much more likely to expand it later on, and potentially split into separate development and testing sprints.

I've worked with many change teams around the world who apply the idea of using sprints. In one case, one of the agile coaches in this enterprise organization was working on a *change user story* for a year: *"as a PMO, I want an agile governance process so I can govern agile processes and teams"*

Sounds good in theory, but over a year and several PowerPoints later, nothing changed. While chunking work into sprints is a good idea, it still requires you think different about what those chunks are. Remember, sprints come from the Scrum framework, and the goal of a sprint is to deliver something of value to the customer.

ADAPTING THE 3RD PRINCIPLE TO CHANGE

Using these questions as a guide, how would you adapt the third agile principle to change?

1. What are we delivering if the change isn't about building software?
2. What is a reasonable period to show tangible results?
3. Outcomes for change may come much later, what could we deliver that demonstrates progress and that we're on the right track?
4. How do we avoid the trap of long feedback cycles because we know tangible outcomes will take a long time?

CROSS-FUNCTIONAL COLLABORATION

Business people and developers must work together daily throughout the project.

* * *

*A*gile Value: Individuals and Interactions over Processes and Tools

Agile has never been an IT thing, and I still can't believe that some organizations I work with don't see that. People think it means that business people and developers are stapled together working feverishly with each other for eight straight hours every day.

This principle is about fast decision making.

Suppose business people and developers don't work together daily. Work gets delayed because developers make assumptions about features, and by the time the business people notice, it's too hard and costly to change.

Here's a real-world example:

One of my old clients was a large financial institution that was structured in a traditional way. There were IT business analysts (BAs) and, uh, *business* business analysts (business BAs) who reported to different customers and stakeholders. The IT BAs have their objectives (on time, on budget), and the business BAs have different objectives (KPI's, business metrics to meet etc.)

Because of this weird dynamic, it took me three months to persuade the business BAs to let the IT BAs, and optionally the rest of the Scrum team, attend the regular customer and stakeholder review meetings. The magic happened in the first session when the business BAs saw how valuable it was to have the IT BAs team talk directly with real customers and stakeholders.

As a reminder, the sprint review in Scrum is generally where that interaction happens, but on huge program involving many people, sometimes having an end of sprint review and a different dedicated stakeholder/customer review is a good idea.

ADAPTING THE 4TH PRINCIPLE TO CHANGE

Using these questions as a guide, how would you adapt the fourth agile principle to change?

1. What problems are being caused by delays in decision making?
2. What structures are in place that prevent cross-

functional collaboration? (A common one is the organizational structure.)

3. Is *working together daily* overkill? What's a reasonable alternative?
4. What ceremonies exist, or which ones should we create, that would allow us to shorten decision making cycles?

INTRINSIC MOTIVATION

Build projects around motivated individuals. Give them the environment and support they need, and trust them to get the job done.

* * *

*A*gile Value: Individuals and Interactions over Processes and Tools

If you are familiar with me or my work, you'll know that my path was shaped by the Amplify Your Effectiveness (AYE) conference. It was a week-long experience for no more than 74 people which keeps it intimate, hosted by the late Jerry Weinberg, Esther Derby, Don Gray, Johanna Rothman, and Steve Smith.

Johanna had run a *finding yourself* session one evening where we explored our patterns through a timeline chart of ups and downs. I discovered that my pattern is one of exploration. That is, I will never be the 20-year employee, I will always challenge the status quo, and I have a low tolerance for corporate BS. Plainly stated, I'm a terrible employee which is why I've been working for myself for 20 years.

In that session, I told Johanna that I thought I wanted to do what she does at some point down the road. The advice she gave me? Start writing. She said that it would help me find my voice, what's important to me, and where I want to go. And she was right.

The blog I mentioned in an earlier chapter that started called *More Agile Than Agile* was designed to not limit myself to just agile-related topics. Great companies evolve by looking through a wide lens, not a telescopic one, so I took the same approach with my blog.

I wrote about using Mastering the Rockefeller Habits at an organization where I worked as a Scrum Master and Product Owner. I also wrote about team dynamics, customer experience, product development, lean startup and more.

The key to this principle is understanding what motivates you. I chose to start writing because I took Johanna's advice based on asking her what could help me achieve my goals. That unlocked my intrinsic motivation versus having someone try to motivate me to write with some external push, or reward.

ADAPTING THE 5TH PRINCIPLE TO CHANGE

Using these questions as a guide, how would you adapt the 5th agile principle to change?

1. How do you find the people motivated to be part of the change?
2. What could be de-motivating people?
3. What help and support do they need?
4. What in the environment is blocking them?
5. Trust is a loaded word; what happens if they make mistakes?

TOUCH OVER TECHNOLOGY

The most efficient and effective method of conveying information to and within a development team is face-to-face conversation.

* * *

*A*gile Value: Individuals and Interactions over Processes and Tools

If you don't follow me on any social media network, you might be unaware of how this book came to be. It poured out of my brain during a few days in the summer of 2019, and I promptly forgot about it.

While restoring a computer backup in the following summer, I found it again. When I looked at it, I thought, what the heck, I'll let Grammarly be my copyeditor (sorry, Julia![1]), and do the least amount of work to get it into production.

The difference in my view of this principle today is the COVID-19 pandemic. I've been working for myself primarily since 2001, so not a whole lot has changed for me in my daily life, but every change agent I know has more or less mentioned that their change initiatives stalled due to the pandemic.

The pandemic has made it harder to get the attention of people and teams because they're exhausted with online meetings for their day-to-day work and there is no energy left for the change.

In some cases, it's because of budget problems. Plenty of organizations lost revenue and simply couldn't pay the change consultants anymore.

Another challenge is the lack of physical connection so visualizing work is much more difficult. As an example, while working in a large bank inside a division of 1600 employees that was starting an agile transformation, the VP asked me what they should do first.

I said *"visualize the work because if you can't see the work, you can't manage it"*. I'm reasonably sure I stole that from Jon Stahl[2]. Visualize first, and that will point out what the right problems are to solve. So we did, and it served its purpose. This is still possible with tools, but it's much harder to do and that makes change move even slower.

That VP was based in another country, so he visited for a week once a month. It was funny how differently people behaved when he was around. He was a great guy, one of the best and most supportive VPs I've ever worked with. He loved the information radiators and it motivated the people around him to use them. The pandemic has taken that energy away.

ADAPTING THE 6TH PRINCIPLE TO CHANGE

Using these questions as a guide, how would you adapt the 6th agile principle to change?

1. Who would be your development team stakeholders? The change team? Other people affected by the change?
2. What's the risk of not having face-to-face interaction?
3. How disruptive and logistically difficult would it be? (Hint: Never take the easy way out because it's a cultural norm. I worked in a large telecom where I could see all the people in one area of the floor in their cubes attending the SAME online meeting because it was easier to multi-task.)

ADAPTABLE METRICS

Working software is the primary measure of progress.

* * *

*A*gile **Value:** Working Software over Comprehensive Documentation

There are a couple of interesting parts to this principle. First, the word *primary* shows that it's not the only measure. Second, *progress* means going forward, not outcomes.

We get far too hung up on binary outcomes and solitary measurements when it comes to change. That's why people still toss around the 70% failure stat[1]. If you're working on replacing a technology where you'll be decommissioning the old one, *percent adoption* doesn't matter. Everyone will have to no matter what, so why continue using it as a measurement?

In software projects, it's easier to see progress because something tangible is delivered. In change, however, the deliverables are often invisible and outcomes are delayed. So sometimes we make up meaningless metrics just to have *something* when it might be better to have anecdotal evidence and stories that tell us we're going in the right direction.

The key with using this principle is to find the right balance of diagnostics and measurements, and change them when they stop being useful.

When change is newly emerging, diagnostics and short feedback loops are important. Later, when we know more and have more certainty, we can refine these metrics based on the outcomes we seek.

This doesn't mean you should skip having outcome measurements at the start, you just don't need to focus on them. A great example is the *earned value* metric. It's a made up metric to make us feel good about progress. There is _zero_ value delivered in projects that use sequential processes, also known as the dreaded waterfall. All of the value is earned when it's in the customers hands.

By contrast, following an iterative approach preached by all agile processes, there is value delivered consistently sprint after sprint. That means if the project is canceled for any reason, there is something of use to the customer and not just a bunch of unfinished documents.

This is why I don't like scorecards and playbooks, at least not in the traditional sense. They're static, prescriptive and don't consider the context.

If we start accepting that we don't know, yet, we can adapt metrics over time.

I worked with a 100-person organization that wanted me to tell them how they would measure my effectiveness as a coach. I told them that any hard evidence like escaped defects and customer satisfaction, would happen after I was already gone since I was there on a short contract.

I suggested they post a sign in the lobby with how much they're paying me and ask everyone I interacted with these questions:

- How often do you work with Jason: 0 = not at all, 5 = everyday
- How much do you feel our organization got our money's worth: 0 = ask for a refund, 5 = what a bargain!
- They didn't go for it, but we did use a modified NPS which asked:
- How valuable was it having Jason as a coach? (0 to 10) Why?

The knock against NPS always seems to be that it's just a number, but it's easy enough to ask people why they gave the number they did. Long story short, the measurement we used was simply anecdotal evidence to the tune of: *"Jason helped us <do this> and that saved us about a week's worth of work"*

ADAPTING THE 7TH PRINCIPLE TO CHANGE

Using these questions as a guide, how would you adapt the 7th agile principle to change?

- What is the change equivalent of "working software"?
- How do you separate "demonstrating progress" with people's need for ROI and other lagging success indicators?
- While "working software" is the primary measure of progress, what are others?
- When and how would you evolve your metrics over time?

ADAPTING TO THE PACE

Agile processes promote sustainable development. The sponsors, developers, and users should be able to maintain a constant pace indefinitely.

* * *

*A*gile **Value**: Working Software over Comprehensive Documentation

Simply put, this principle is about sustainable pace. It's unfortunate that many see that Scrum uses the word "sprint" and assumes that it refers only to speed.

Sustainable pace is about having the ability to maintain a constant pace indefinitely. *Theory U*[1] refers to this as a heartbeat.

In my book *Lean Change Management*[2], I talked about how The Commission was undergoing three massive changes simultaneously:

1. Agile transformation
2. Mass layoffs
3. A huge technology migration

It was a perfect storm analogous to changing the engine of the plane while flying.

This principle relates to what traditionalists call *change fatigue*. There's too much change happening and people can't absorb it. Misalignment and lack of cohesion are the usual culprits, but there are others.

In larger organizations with agile coaching, change, organizational development (OD), and HR teams, lack of cohesion happens when each department is working on their own change in isolation, even though there is usually overlap.

For example, agile coaches often focus on happy team members, while HR folks may be running an employee satisfaction program simultaneously. The team is getting bombarded by surveys, conflicting information, and sometimes, conflicting objectives.

It's essential to understand what else is going on in the organization that might be distracting people from dedicating time to the change.

ADAPTING THE 8TH PRINCIPLE TO CHANGE

Using these questions as a guide, how would you adapt the 8th agile principle to change?

1. What's the organization's natural pace of change?
2. What day-to-day work is competing with the change?
3. Who's overloaded with work?
4. Where is the 'push' for the change coming from?

ADAPTABLE CHANGE PROCESS

Continuous attention to technical excellence and good design enhances agility.

* * *

*A*gile **Value**: Working Software over Comprehensive Documentation

In a software context, this principle is about how delivery teams do their work. Technical excellence includes using all of the Extreme Programming (XP) tools like test-driven development, collective code ownership, pair programming, and more.

In the late 90s and early 2000s, when I started my own web development company, I used Active Server Pages (ASP), which used Visual Basic (VB) Script. Without getting too technical, ASP is not a managed code language and the code is contained inside web pages. That means there is no refactoring magic or intelligent code tools built that can be used changes safely. If I added one field of data in one script, I had to search every ASP page to find where I wanted to use it or change it.

I would accidentally break things on the websites without knowing it, and trying to fix it added many hours to each project. I was sick of spending all that extra effort so I built my own approach to testing and logging. Then, when I made a change in one spot, I could quickly test the most important parts of the application. It wasn't nearly as slick as some of testing automation tools of today, but it was good enough.

Without focusing on good technical practices, there was simply no way to be agile, and that's the massive mistake many organizations make when they transition to agile. They forget that the process is simple; the technical stuff is substantially harder.

Adapting this principle to change will be tough. Hopefully, you're doing these exercises before I show you how I adapted them! It's more fun that way (I think!)

ADAPTING THE 9TH PRINCIPLE TO CHANGE

Using these questions as a guide, how would you adapt the 9th agile principle to change?

1. Agile vs Agile: what's being disciplined, and what's just changing stuff whenever we feel like it?
2. What's the change equivalent of *technical excellence* and *good design*

3. How do you know if you have achieved the change equivalent of "technical excellence" and "good design"?

KEEP IT SIMPLE

Simplicity — the art of maximizing the amount of work not done — is essential.

* * *

*A*gile **Value**: Responding to Change over Following a Plan

You're probably tired of hearing my AYE stories, but too bad! Here's another one!

Jerry Weinberg ran a session titled *How to Say No*, and it was so popular that most, if not all, attendees went to it. This was at a time when he was recovering from cancer, was in a wheelchair, and his speaking voice was quite weak.

I remember sitting in a circle with everyone, and he opened with, *"I'd like you all to say no."* We replied in unison, *"No."* He proceeded with, *"What was so hard about that?"*

He invited everyone to think of a time that they wanted to say no, but said yes instead. He asked for two volunteers; one would be the star; the other would be an actor representing the person the star wanted to say no to. The two volunteers sat in the middle of the circle and had a conversation while Jerry coached the star.

Jerry had a knack for making complex situations simple. This was a lesson in congruence. That is, understanding what the other person is asking in a certain context, but also staying true to yourself and what you need.

For agile delivery teams, saying no isn't a finality. It's more of a *not-yet* than a no, and it's a way to prioritize work. I've seen enough projects with seventeen number one priorities. (Seriously.) Most of the time, these priorities are what-if scenarios or untested assumptions. The iterative nature of agile makes it possible to defer decision making by focusing on the highest priority items.

That means switching he conversation to prioritization instead of focusing on the negative of saying no. In change work, this helps us avoid trying every idea at once by throwing ALL THE CHANGES at a team or organization, hoping that a few stick.

ADAPTING THE 10TH PRINCIPLE TO CHANGE

Using these questions as a guide, how would you adapt the 10th principle to change?

1. How do you say no to stakeholders who want you to push for more change when you know the time isn't right?
2. How do you prioritize change work?
3. How much complexity do you add to your change or change process through untested or unvalidated assumptions?
4. How do you minimize your change process so you can focus on people?

THE PEOPLE WHO WRITE THE PLAN, DON'T FIGHT THE PLAN

The best architectures, requirements, and designs emerge from self-organizing teams.

* * *

*A*gile Value: Individuals and interactions over processes and tools

"The people who write the plan don't fight the plan."

This is my favourite quote from Jill Forbes. She was working for National Leasing and was using ideas from *Lean Change Management*[1].

A pivotal moment for her that moved the change forward was when she ran a change canvas[2] session with the manager. It helped transfer the ownership of the change from the change people to the people affected.

This is where the power of cross-functional teams comes into play. In Scrum, the team has people with all the necessary skills to do the work. That might mean having developers, designers, CX/UX, testers and architects all on the same team.

The key is having T-shaped people, which is quickly evolving to bridge-shaped people:

- T-shaped people have deep skill in one area and a smattering of other skills
- Bridge-shaped people have deep skills in a couple, or few areas and smattering of other skills.

A Java developer who only knows Java very well and has surface knowledge of a few other things is T-shaped. A full-stack developer that knows Java, HTML, CSS, and Javascript very well, but also knows about database technology and infrastructure is bridge-shaped.

Some people think this means they need multi-skilled people who can do everything. Not true. It simply means having more than one specialized skill so self-organizing is more effective.

A challenge moving towards a culture that values bridge-shaped people is the roles and titles handed out to people. I've seen team members labeled as a Senior Java III Developer who flat out refuse to do any testing, or learn other technologies because they're measured on much Java code they can crank out.

I worked with one organization that didn't have this problem. Team members were simply called *builders* - they built stuff. Some skewed toward testing, some more toward development, but there were enough multi-skilled people to allow them to spread the work out. They weren't as reliant on the one developer who knew how to change that one messy part of the code.

Multiple brains are better than one, a team is more likely to figure out the right way forward when they're not handed a solution.

ADAPTING THE 11TH PRINCIPLE TO CHANGE

Using these questions as a guide, how would you adapt the 11th agile principle to change?

1. What's the change equivalent of architecture, requirements, and design? (Hint: don't take the easy way out and say *the plan* - we all know some type of plan with a certain level of detail is important.)
2. Which teams are self-organizing? The change team? The people affected by the change?
3. What guardrails are in place to protect self-organization from slipping into chaos?

INSPECT AND ADAPT

*At regular intervals, the team reflects on how to become more effective,
then tunes, and adjusts its behaviour accordingly.*

* * *

*A*gile **Value**: responding to change over following a plan

In a word, retrospectives. My friend and colleague, Declan Whelan likes to say that if you can only do one agile practice, pick retrospectives because no matter what process you follow, you'll improve things over time.

While working in a 100-person organization with a flat hierarchy, the CTO and Scrum Master complained that the team would never make improvements, and retrospectives were useless. In reality, they were useless because of a lack of ownership by the team.

The CTO and Scrum Master were deciding on what to improve instead of letting the team figure it out. When I facilitated their next retrospective, I asked the CTO and Scrum Master to observe and not say anything.

They were shocked to hear the ideas the team came up with. These were ideas they would never have thought of, but thought were excellent ideas. The first idea they picked to improve was the daily standup. The stand-ups took too long and had too much detail for the team, so we talked about the standup's purpose. In Scrum, it's a ceremony to plan a daily goal that contributes to the sprint goal.

The team decided to draft a daily goal on their whiteboard and try it for a sprint. After the first sprint, they thought it didn't help much, so we refined it and dug deeper. The real problem was that they didn't do a thorough enough sprint planning, so details that usually come up, didn't come up until mid-way or near the end of the sprint.

After a few sprints the team learned that they controlled what to improve and how to do it.

ADAPTING THE 12TH PRINCIPLE TO CHANGE

Using these questions as a guide, how would you adapt the 12th agile principle to change?

1. How often does your change team reflect and refine your change process?

2. How are stakeholders involved?
3. What about people affected by the change?

PRIORITIZING YOUR PRINCIPLES

Organizational change is like a Rubik's cube made with colour-changing LEDs. It might get harder to solve with each move you make.

* * *

There are so many factors that affect how you approach change:

- What type of change is this? A re-org? An agile transformation? A system implementation? An innovation program?
- What's the attitude of the leaders?
- What's the overall culture like? What about sub-cultures within the organization?
- What are the existing organizational norms?
- What's the structure of the organization?
- How does influence work?

While we've looked at the four values and twelve principles so far, we may need to focus on some more than others.

There's a great game called Pocket-Sized Principles1 that helps teams internalize and deeply understand the twelve principles, and here are the basics of how it works:

1. Give a group of people the twelve principles.
2. Ask them to summarize each statement in three words or less.

The objective is for the group of people to coalesce around a common understanding of the principle.

Over the last decade, I tweaked the game for organizations who wanted to either transform to agile or become more agile with their change management practices.

After they complete the first part, I would ask these questions:

- Which of the twelve principles would be the three that are most important for you?
- Which of the twelve principles would be the three that would be the hardest to follow?
- Which of the twelve principles are ones that you believe you live by today, and why?

The questions would vary on the context, but the goal is to look for congruence. Every organization says, and wants to believe, they live by ethical, positive values, and then proceed to behave in the opposite way.

A great example is the statement, *we value people* - followed by behaviours that match a missing amendment - *provided they are at their desks for 40-hours a week and adhering to performance management objectives.*

WE ALL WANT THE SAME THING

I was asked to spend a week training an R&D division of 200 people who had been practicing agile for a year, but never formalized their practices.

I ran this exercise with the leaders and all the team members, and here were the results:

A FEW THINGS STAND OUT.

First, why is Principle 8, sustainable pace, the most challenging, but not valuable?

They answered that people feel overworked, but they love the rush. Anyone who's worked in a startup knows that feeling. I do too. I've worked for many and that feeling is just incredible. Unsustainable, but incredible.

Second, why is the 12th principle, retrospectives, the most challenging and valuable?

They answered that they do retrospectives and get some value, but there's no one facilitating them, so the most dominant voice wins.

POINTING FINGERS

Plenty of organizations do this. The people at the top think the problem is with the teams, and the teams think the problem is the people at the top.

But they both want the same thing. Everyone wants to feel appreciated, valued, and part of something.

After running this exercise with the leaders and the team, it was clear they wanted the same thing, so now it became a choice:

- Fix the teams with agile.
- Have more meaningful dialogue to move forward as an organization.

Some managers chose the second option, while others chose the first option. Some didn't do anything. This isn't a knock on the people; I remember my first director position, I was not ready for it, so I wouldn't have been able to have these conversations without a coach.

WHICH ARE YOUR TOP PRIORITIES?

In the opening of this chapter, I showed a few factors that must be considered for how you approach change.

Hopefully, you did the workbook exercises, but if not, go through the twelve principles and pick the top three that would be the most important for you to focus on to create a more agile approach to change.

Then, pick the top three that would be the hardest to follow, given your context.

Share what you come up with and see what others did at changeagility.org

PART III - MY TAKE - MODERN CHANGE MANAGEMENT PRINCIPLES

A while back, I tweeted that adding the word *agile* to a function — agile marketing, agile change management, agile testing, agile sales, agile personal productivity — is missing the point of agile.

It was probably in response to a ridiculous article about *how to transform your sales team into an agile sales team* and I reacted.

As usual, someone choosing to hide behind a phoney Twitter handle who clearly knows who I am replied, *"Those in glass houses..."* as an obvious jab at my first book, *Lean Change Management*.

I replied, *"Well, I called originally it 'How Jason Likes to Work,' but focus groups told me no one would buy it."* This book is the book about how I like to work. It's not about giving you a framework, or method to follow, it's about conveying the thought process behind how I go about being an agent of change, based on making the most of the core values of agile.

HOW JASON LIKES TO WORK™

I've lost track of how many times I've been given a scenario and then asked how I would handle it. This book describes the method to my madness and shows you how I answered the questions about how to adapt each agile principle to change in Part II .

If you've been doing the exercises up to now, you'll have a better idea of what I'll talk about next. I was inspired to do that through an organizational change course I took through MIT.

It was a mix of online and self-study, and I loved the format. The professor would introduce a concept, give the attendees a statement or short scenario, and ask us to write down what we would do and what we thought might happen.

You **had** to do this before continuing, and after you submitted, there was a short video of the professor explaining how the story turned out.

I loved the idea of applying what I already knew and then having him bridge the gap with the models they were teaching, so I thought it would work well in this book too.

That is also one of the main reasons created changewayfinder.com as an ongoing, living accompaniment to this book.

There's only so much I can put into it, but there's much more the overall change community can add to it. Don't forget to check it out once you've finished this book.

MIND THE PEOPLE

Our highest priority is to satisfy the customer through early and continuous delivery of valuable software.

* * *

WHAT'S MY *HIGHEST PRIORITY*?

My highest priority is to help people make sense of their context so they can figure out options for moving forward.

HOW DO I FULFILL THAT PRIORITY?

I default to a coaching stance. That is, I will help people discover options without coercing or influencing or providing unsolicited advice.

WHAT'S THE CHANGE EQUIVALENT OF *VALUABLE SOFTWARE?*

For me, it's delivering an *aha!* moment measured by a fist-or-five feedback session. E.g. *"Considering this session, how valuable was it for you from 0 to 5? Hold up your hand, a fist means 0, 5 fingers means 5, and if it's a 1, please play nicely!"*

WHAT WOULD *EARLY AND CONTINUOUS* MEAN IN A CHANGE CONTEXT?

For me, this would align to the natural pace of change in the organization and how much uncertainty the change brings.

* * *

HOW I REFRAME THE 1ST PRINCIPLE

Our highest priority is to satisfy the customer through early and continuous delivery of valuable software.

MY HIGHEST PRIORITY is to help clients make sense of their context through frequent facilitated conversations and sense-making sessions.

HOW IT GUIDES MY ACTIONS

- When in doubt, have a conversation.
- When asked to create a *better plan* or roadmap, do it co-creatively.
- Answer questions with stories so the client can relate the story to what it could look like in their organization.
- Connect clients to other clients. Once an enterprise client I was working with wanted to re-organize their space and they wanted me, the agile expert, to do it. Instead, I took them to a previous client to show them what an awesome design could look like.

WELCOME CHANGE

Welcome changing requirements, even late in development. Agile processes harness change for the customer's competitive advantage.

* * *

WHAT ARE THE *CHANGING REQUIREMENTS?*

For me, it's engagement scope. I go where help is needed, and don't worry about not being allowed to help a particular team. This also means challenging the sunk-cost fallacy if the change is about a new system implementation. I believe it's my responsibility to leave options open as long as possible.

IS *LATE IN DEVELOPMENT* THE *LAST RESPONSIBLE MOMENT* OR IRRESPONSIBLE?

Agile uses the phrase *last responsible moment* to avoid making decisions too soon. There's a fine line between that and being irresponsible. For me, it's about helping people make good enough decisions with the information available.

If we believe it's very late for a specific change, we must still explore the possibility instead of avoiding a hard conversation.

WHAT ABOUT OUR CHANGE PROCESS PREVENTS COURSE CORRECTION?

Traditional change management thinking tries to separate change management from project management. That's what often puts us in a position of following the plan when adapting to change is more relevant.

WHAT COULD *CHANGE* ABOUT HOW WE DO CHANGE THAT WOULD MAKE US MORE ADAPTABLE?

Are the feedback loops between what is happening for the people affected by the change versus the stakeholders too long? Do we have too much process for the sake of having process?

My rule is to have a minimum viable change process that lets us focus on people, not process.

HOW I REFRAME THE 2ND PRINCIPLE

Welcome changing requirements, even late in development. Agile processes harness change for the customer's competitive advantage.

LEAVE options open as long as possible and detach from the outcome so your opinion doesn't get in the way of what's best for the client.

* * *

HOW IT GUIDES MY ACTIONS

- **Congruence**: When clients want to change things and you've spent a lot of time trying to make it work, it's ok to say, *"I don't like this...I spent a lot of time doing XYZ."* Be true to what you need, but stick around to negotiate.
- **Exploration of options**: This is definitely more art than science. You could go crazy with keeping things too loose. I like to have enough insights to create well-thought out options, and eventually experiments that don't cover everything, but helps us make a well-informed choice to move forward
- **Consequence of actions**: Late changes have consequences, and I don't mean *the project schedule says we're late.* I'm talking about all the refactoring, retraining, and inevitable confusion that'll happen when the organization decides to make a strong change in

direction for the change. It's important to talk about how bad the visibility of changing direction might be. One problem might be that people poured their heart and soul into something that the leaders have now decided isn't valuable. It's demotivating!

SHORT FEEDBACK LOOPS

Deliver working software frequently, from a couple of weeks to a couple of months, with a preference to the shorter timescale.

* * *

WHAT ARE WE DELIVERING IF THE CHANGE ISN'T ABOUT BUILDING SOFTWARE?

a common answer to this is, *we're delivering behaviour or mindset changes.* That can get us into a whole bunch of trouble. We'll start looking for ways to measure behaviours and mindsets, which borders on being the change *police* instead of change *agents*.

I like to start as loose as possible to show some type of tangible delivery or progress, including:

- Asking people early on, *"Given we've been doing <this change> for <this time period>, on a scale from 0 to 5, do you think we're headed in the right direction?"*
- When people don't see progress, I ask, *"What evidence do you need to see we are moving forward?"*

Change agents should **never** own the outcome of a change. Sometimes the organization expects everyone to show proof that they're doing work and, more often than not, what we do generates invisible outcomes.

This comes down to expectations, making sure you've set the proper expectations, and having short feedback loops early on in the change.

WHAT IS A REASONABLE PERIOD TO SHOW TANGIBLE RESULTS?

This is very difficult with agile transformations or multi-year programs. I worked with a government organization that was working on a three-year SAP implementation that often showed no progress for months at a time, but was indeed moving forward.

The change lead put up a big visible wall and ran a weekly standup for the stakeholders. That was it, and it was good enough at the time. He didn't throw out their existing processes or try to change people. He had a short weekly conversation to make all of the invisible work visible.

WHAT COULD WE DELIVER THAT DEMONSTRATES PROGRESS?

If we understand that visible progress is slow early on, we need a better way to provide that evidence. That could include:

- Outcomes from experiments.
- Early feedback that provokes a discussion.
- The sentiment, happiness, and stress level trends.

We all want evidence-based change management and desperately want to believe it's a science.

Early on, anecdotal evidence is enough to make decisions. If we know after two weeks that everyone loves the new way of doing things despite the stress and unknowns, that helps us move forward.

HOW DO WE AVOID THE TRAP OF LONG FEEDBACK CYCLES BECAUSE WE KNOW TANGIBLE OUTCOMES WILL TAKE A LONG TIME?

This is a trap conservative change agents fall into because instead of showing fuzzy, anecdotal evidence that *something* is happening, they decide to not show anything except for more PowerPoints.

It's easy to put off uncomfortable conversations by increasing the length of feedback cycles. It's sort of like the idea of having green status reports when the project starts.

It makes sense that we have no realized risks because we haven't done anything yet, but isn't that worse? Try these:

- **Start projects red**: My friend and colleague, Andrew Annett says that at the start of a project you have a full wallet and an empty brain. Start your projects red and talk with stakeholders about the three most important things you're doing this week to move it towards green.
- **Feedback on the feedback loop**: Have a short weekly retrospective and do a 0-5 satisfaction survey on fingers with your change team about how effective your work cycles are.
- **How short is too short?** There's a chance you'll annoy people by having feedback loops that are too short. Use your eyes, ears, and brain to stay perceptive about how people feel and how they react to what might be perceived as useless meetings for feedback that don't accomplish anything.

A GREAT QUESTION I like to ask is,"*Do you think we're going too slow? Too fast? Is there anything I should be doing that I'm not doing right now?*"

HOW I REFRAME THE 3RD PRINCIPLE

Deliver working software frequently, from a couple of weeks to a couple of months, with a preference to the shorter timescale.

MAKE the invisible visible knowing that change doesn't change as fast as software features.

HOW IT GUIDES MY ACTIONS

Asking for too much feedback, too frequently, can get annoying pretty fast. My rules on feedback are:

- Understand what other changes might be competing for people's time and attention. I'll often reach out to other people to see how we can merge or align our change efforts, especially if there is overlap.
- I am bullish on visualization, and do anything I can to visualize work in-person, or virtually in order to have a *single source of truth*
- Balance anecdotal evidence of progress with outcomes (this is very important early on.)

CROSS-FUNCTIONAL COLLABORATION

Business people and developers must work together daily throughout the project.

* * *

WHAT PROBLEMS ARE BEING CAUSED BY DELAYS IN DECISION MAKING?

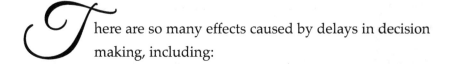here are so many effects caused by delays in decision making, including:

- Finding out too late the change is the wrong one, which leads to pushing it through anyway due to the sunk-cost fallacy.
- Apathy in organizations where the people are desperate for the leaders to make decisions but the leaders want to

push decision making down. After a while, teams give and end up making choices without being transparent about how the decision came to be.

In Johanna Rothman's fantastic book, *Managing Your Project Portfolio*[1], she tells a story about working as a program manager. She had too many projects to get done and needed them prioritized. She asked. And asked. And asked again.

Finally, she said something like, *"I have decided to prioritize these projects in this way for these reasons in absence of a decision from you."*

The word *decision* has a sense of finality to it, but that doesn't mean we can change our mind later. We just need some decision to take a step forward.

WHAT STRUCTURES ARE IN PLACE THAT PREVENT CROSS-FUNCTIONAL COLLABORATION?

Most of the time, organizational structures get in the way. A friend of mine who worked as an agile coach in a large telecom was forbidden by the director of the division to talk to any team that wasn't in his scope.

While this is childish, if you look deeper, there's something else going on here. The worst thing that can happen to leaders is that they're the last to know about something that happened in their department.

Maybe you're thinking, *"Childish?? Gee, that's not supposed to be written in a professional book about change management."* To which I respond, *"C'mon. We hire smart, capable people and treat them like children."* Calling out childish behaviour is a way to shock the system into change. Sometimes it works, sometimes it gets you fired, but stupid things like this is a clear sign the organization is never going to change.

I worked in one organization where multiple teams were working on the same program. Each team wanted to charge the other team's department for attending their standup meetings to coordinate work between the teams. So they decided not to collaborate instead to save money.

This is another childish and stupid behaviour, but one that is engrained in many organizational cultures, especially in some enterprise organizations.

While you do need to respect the structures to a certain degree, you need to challenge some of this stupid behaviour.

IS *WORK TOGETHER DAILY* OVERKILL? WHAT'S A REASONABLE ALTERNATIVE?

Don't confuse work together daily with thinking that a full re-organization needs to happen.

- Ask the teams if it's ok to attend their stand-ups, create your own standup for the change team, and ask the program lead to attend it.
- Repurpose your existing meetings to follow a daily standup format, or a lean coffee format.

There are so many ways to solve this problem, and at the heart of it is finding the right cadence that allows you to make decisions sooner.

WHAT CEREMONIES EXIST, OR WHICH ONES SHOULD WE CREATE, THAT WOULD ALLOW US TO SHORTEN DECISION-MAKING CYCLES?

I touched on this in the last point. All organizations have regular meetings, and often they add more when a change is happening.

Create a ritual inventory[2] and figure out how to repurpose existing ones before adding new ones.

Perhaps the best story I have about this principle is working with a multinational organization with change agents worldwide. Some were agile coaches, some were change consultants, and some were managers.

Instead of competing with each other, as so many functional teams do, they worked together and met three times a month to support each other.

HOW I REFRAME THE 4TH PRINCIPLE

Business people and developers must work together daily throughout the project.

CHANGE MANAGERS, agile coaches, OD/HR, and managers need to coalesce efforts by creating cohesion between competing change initiatives

HOW IT GUIDES MY ACTIONS

This is simple for me. I like to know what else is happening in the organization. It's easy to claim ignorance when there are competing change coming from another department, but it's your duty to ask questions:

- What else is happening now? I always seek to understand what other forces are competing with what I've been asked to do.
- What other changes happened before this? It's important to understand the history. If the change has been tried before, starting with a retrospective could uncover valuable information.
- Who is *doing* change management today? There might be multiple consulting firms doing changes, and possibly internal change teams, as well as managers and people on teams. I will often try to piggy-back my efforts and align with other people.
- I encourage informal change networks, especially by linking agile coaches to OD, HR, and change teams. They might not need to work together daily, but they should sync up every so often.

INTRINSIC MOTIVATION

Build projects around motivated individuals. Give them the environment and support they need, and trust them to get the job done.

* * *

HOW DO YOU FIND THE PEOPLE MOTIVATED TO BE PART OF THE CHANGE?

Generally speaking, the most vocal people are motivated. That might mean they're incredibly supportive or a skeptic. That's the energy you're going to need to move the change forward.

Keep your eyes open for the movers, movables, and immovables that have energy, and tap into it.

For example, in the organization I wrote about in *Lean Change Management*, we started with lean coffee sessions, and the business analysts kept showing up each week. We knew we had strongly motivated people, so we worked very closely with them.

WHAT COULD BE DEMOTIVATING PEOPLE?

Never underestimate the feeling of having choices taken away. If we push change too much, people can appear demotivated because they don't feel they have a choice.

Another issue could be incongruence. For example, the leaders want the agile transformation to succeed, but they won't allow business people to talk directly with developers.

Maybe the team's most influential personality is against the change, but everyone else supports it, but doesn't feel they can speak up.

Never leap to resistance on an individual level; look for systemic effects and dynamics first.

WHAT HELP AND SUPPORT DO THEY NEED?

Part of this is your intuition. While working as a Scrum Master, I found one team member that said at the daily standup, *"Yesterday I worked on X, today I'll keep working X. No blockers"*

That happened for three straight days, so I knew he was blocked, and it was my job to talk to him afterwards to see if he needed help.

Support isn't just helping and supporting people as the change agent. It's also about working on blockers in the system that people can't resolve on their own.

In one organization, the director was unaware of why the team kept needing more time and budget to finish a large program. As the coach, I asked the team if I could *break protocol* and bring him our cumulative flow (CFD) chart .

The CFD chart showed that for every feature we finished, the business added two more. I told the team it was likely they would get in trouble even I was the one who broke protocol, but they said it was ok.

Be clear about how you can help, and let the people decide so you don't seem like a *fixer*.

WHAT IN THE ENVIRONMENT IS BLOCKING THEM?

We always assume people aren't motivated when we don't see change happening. Sometimes they are motivated, but the change is too hard, there's too much day-job stuff going on, or there are too many obstacles.

A perfect example is when organizations undergoing an agile transformation rename existing teams as Scrum teams and keep the people assigned to seven projects.

When the team doesn't deliver, we assume they're resisting or are unmotivated. The worst I saw was an eight-person project with one project manager, one developer, and six business analysts in three different time zones. Here's the fun part; 8% of the developer's time was allocated to the project. I was tasked with making that project agile which was a pointless endeavour because no one was focused on what needed to be delivered.

All organizations get stuck somehow. From my experience, it's usually because of systemic factors. Of course, some people may also not be motivated or think the change is stupid, which doesn't help matters.

Welcome to the exciting world of being an agent of change!

TRUST IS A LOADED WORD; WHAT HAPPENS IF THEY MAKE MISTAKES?

I learned a great tip from Patrick Lencioni's book, *Getting Naked*[1]. One of his naked consulting model's principles is to take the bullet for the client.

I use the phrase *get out of jail free* instead, but since both of those metaphors are negative, I may have to come up with a more positive one for my next book!

No matter, ignore all of this nonsense around accepting failure, *failing better*, or whatever other trendy statement you might see. They've never been useful to me. This is why I promote Jurgen Appelo's celebration grid[2]. It focuses on the massive grey area between success and failure, but at its core, you learn from all experiences.

It's more important to let the emotions wear off the alleged failure, and then wipe the slate clean with a rational conversation.

Whenever we faced a problem, one of my favourite managers always liked to say, *"All right people, let's figure out how to get the cow out of the ditch!"* It was a great way to let the team know that yes, we had a problem, but it wasn't the end of the world.

Once again, Jerry Weinberg to the rescue! He once said that the problem isn't the problem, often the *reaction* to the problem is the problem.

A QUICK STORY

Back in 2012, I was a senior agile coach in an organization, and our team had a few junior agile coaches. Our team always worked together as peers, rather than junior/senior coaches, so as long as you don't tell anyone, I can tell you this secret about it.

Senior and *junior* are only division-of-work labels and were an HR way of paying us differently. An example of division-of-work was that only *senior* coaches could talk to the executives. We told our manager that all the *junior* people should have the same title so they could have the same pay because the difference in title isn't helpful for the type of work we were doing.

To help explain this to management, I ran a session called The Product Box[3] for the junior coaches to find out what motivated them. After that, the other senior coach, and I started finding opportunities in the organization that would help them get there. The manager talked to me and the other senior coach, decided to change the titles, but did ask us if that would hurt our sense of status, which was nice. I see how that could be a problem, but it didn't matter to either of us.

After that conversation, everyone was *promoted*, and that was that.

One of the junior coaches told me what I told Johanna many years back at AYE. "I think I want to do what you do." I offered to work with him to co-develop and co-deliver a session at the Agile Alliance conference[4], which, at the time, was the most significant annual agile conference attracting close to 3,000 people.

* * *

HOW I REFRAME THE 5TH PRINCIPLE

Build projects around motivated individuals. Give them the environment and support they need, and trust them to get the job done.

ENABLE THE MOVERS TO do their best work, remove organizational obstacles, and step aside.

* * *

HOW IT GUIDES **my actions**

- **I support the skeptics**: There are always people who seem opposed to the change. It could be they have a better idea, or could mean that they hate their job too.

While I do support them, I don't focus my energy there while traditional change management says you should identify and overcome resistance. It's far too exhausting.

- **Enable the Movers**: On the opposite side of the spectrum, and without getting too political, I act as a shield for the movers. The movers are those people who fully support the change and want to run with it. Sometimes they need an external ally that can take some of the heat.
- **Change My Stance**: While working in a large telecom, we approached the first set of teams as *coaches* because they were highly motivated to try agile practices. When it came time for the next round of teams to come onboard, I asked people from the first round of teams to tell their stories to the new teams. Instead of approaching the 2nd round of teams like a *coach*, I approached them as a *trainer*.

TOUCH OVER TECHNOLOGY

The most efficient and effective method of conveying information to, and within, a development team is face-to-face conversation.

WHO ARE YOUR STAKEHOLDERS?

This principle refers to a development team. Let's assume that means your change team. All change teams I've worked with that wanted to adopt an agile way of doing change had daily stand-ups.

Stakeholders were invited if they wanted the day-to-day details, and sometimes the "daily" standup would happen every other day, or every few days.

The key is to go back to intent. How often does information change? What's the pace of the change? Don't communicate daily if you don't need to.

Face-to-face, even over video is so fast and easy, try it first and adjust as necessary.

What's the risk of not having face-to-face interaction?

This is harder in a post-COVID world. It's not only that face-to-face interaction is sometimes not possible, but it also leads to online exhaustion. When COVID hit, all of the remote experts came online, followed closely by the Zoom fatigue experts warning against overdoing it.

If we operate in a remote culture, is the absence of meaningful dialogue causing problems? Are there too many touch-points?

Sometimes Slack, or other online chat tools are good enough, so, use your best judgement.

HOW DOES THE PACE OF CHANGE DIFFER IN A REMOTE CULTURE?

Again, this is mostly related to living in a post-COVID world. Many change agents I know mention their changes have stalled.

Some feel they need to push through despite the obstacles. While this principle is about face-to-face communication, not being able to have face-to-face communication is a disruption that can help you re-evaluate the change in the first place.

If the pace slows and it doesn't matter, that might be a sign that the change, in its current form, isn't the right thing to do anymore.

HOW DISRUPTIVE AND LOGISTICALLY TRICKY WOULD IT BE?

I worked in yet another large bank that had buildings all over the downtown area. I would intentionally schedule my days to get face-time with people knowing I'd have a lot of walking to do. I'd get some exercise while creating more relationships.

Take the extra effort to build a stronger mental connection. Once myself and 3 other coaches facilitated a large retrospective with forty people in the room, and another 60 or so on a conference call. We synchronized a physical sticky note wall with a virtual one which was a lot of effort, and not something I'd want to do regularly.

Why you ask? Why not simply have everyone be remote? The reason for doing this was to show the internal coaching team possibilities. This organization had a common condition called impossibility-itis. We'd suggest something, they'd reply with, *"that's impossible!!"*

So we needed to show them how to remove their blinders.

A QUICK STORY

Before COVID-19, when we were allowed to leave our homes, I worked with a large telecom where the business people worked in one building, and the IT team in another about 40 km away.

I remember our first sprint review, where the poor Scrum master was on the phone, stalling the business team while the developers ironed out one last bug that would have killed the demo.

In a calm voice, she'd say, *"Thanks for joining everyone, we're just about set up and waiting on a couple of people, so we'll get started in a few minutes."*

Then she'd hit the mute button, lean towards the open conference door, and yell, *"GUYS!!!! IS IT RUNNING YET?!?!?!"*

During one of our retrospectives, the physical separation problem came up, and the team agreed to rotate the location of their planning and sprint review sessions. For the next sprint, the people downtown decided to drive uptown, and the sprint after that, the uptown folks would drive downtown.

You may think this is a waste of time, and you might be right, but that wasn't *your* team or *your* problem, nor mine. They came to this solution because it was best for *them*.

Your team could do this remotely, this team needed to be face-to-face to make a more meaningful connection.

While this principle says face-to-face conversation, that doesn't have to mean in-person. Yes the team I worked with preferred traveling between locations, but if they couldn't do that, video conferencing would be better than nothing.

That's important because I worked in another organization where no one ever turned on their cameras for video calls.

They used one tool for video, and regular conference bridges for audio. You would hear the *beep* that someone joined, but no one would say they joined. It was funny, and sad, to watch the people in the room get anxious asking, *"Uh, who joined? Hello? Did someone join?"*

While that's a perfect sign of a trust problem, again, face-to-face doesn't have to mean in-person. It just means doing whatever we need to in order to see each other as humans.

HOW I REFRAME THE 6TH PRINCIPLE

The most efficient and effective method of conveying information to and within a development team is face-to-face conversation.

Mental closeness matters more than physical closeness. People work together on the change better when they see each other as people and, generally speaking, face-to-face interaction makes that possible.

HOW IT GUIDES MY ACTIONS

- **Establish relationships**: I take time to establish relationships and model the behaviour that aligns with the values and principles of agile.
- **I model the behaviour**: From the story in this chapter, I would always turn on my camera for video calls and announce myself on conference calls. I want everyone else to do that too, especially if it's not the cultural norm.
- **A more human touch**: I use this principle to work on bringing humanity back into the workplace. If people see other people as, well, people, they're more likely to be open to understanding different perspectives.

ADAPTABLE METRICS

Working software is the primary measure of progress.

* * *

WHAT IS THE CHANGE EQUIVALENT OF *WORKING SOFTWARE?*

*T*his is obvious if your change is implementing software! Even so, there are better metrics early, especially with large systems implementation where you generally don't see anything tangible for weeks or months.

Early in a change, I like to use diagnostics and ask, *"what evidence do we have that tells us we're headed in the right direction?"* It doesn't even have to be specific evidence either. Fuzzy data is better than none, IMO! For example:

- Fist of Five: Using a 0 to 5 scale either in-person on fingers or through online surveys if you need feedback from lots of people.
- It's been <this long> since we started doing <this change>, how much better is it so far? 0 = much worse, 5 = much better
- It's been <this long> since we started doing <this change>, do you think as a whole organization we're committed to it?
- These are the outcomes we're after <list outcomes>, do you think what we're focused on will get us there? 0 = we need a serious u-turn, 5 = we're on the right track

There are infinite combinations for these questions. The key is to find the right ones that provide *some* evidence that what we're doing is the right thing, even if we can't see anything tangible yet.

HOW DO YOU SEPARATE "DEMONSTRATING PROGRESS" WITH PEOPLE'S NEED FOR ROI AND OTHER LAGGING SUCCESS INDICATORS?

This is tricky. People love scorecards and measures, and we *think* that's what leaders want. I can promise you, they don't, even if that's what they're asking for.

Leaders and stakeholders, like most people in organizations, are busy. They want data that helps them make decisions.

Everyone wants to believe that the time and money invested in a change is worth it, but ROI and transformational change is like oil and water. They don't mix.

I worked in an organization where the external consultants posted a paper on their website about how this organization used their method and found a 400% productivity increase.

As measured by what? That was omitted from the article.

Of course, this organization easily spent north of $2M on these consultants, so they damn well have better had some ROI!

I'm a bit cynical about metrics because they are so often misused. A good practice I use myself is that if the measurement is easy to come up with and measure, it's probably a lousy measurement because we haven't thought it through.

WHILE *WORKING SOFTWARE* IS THE PRIMARY MEASURE OF PROGRESS, WHAT ARE OTHERS?

I've mentioned this a few times, and it's my job to suggest options and let the organization pick:

- Is the change making people's jobs easier?
- Are people happier?
- Are people paying for the projects more satisfied?
- Are end-users requesting support less?
- Is the stress-level of employees decreasing?
- Are we increasing profits?

Use the Lean Startup pirate metrics (AARRR):

- **Acquisition**: How did customers find us?
- **Activation**: Did they have an excellent first experience?
- **Retention**: Did they come back?
- **Referral**: Did they tell others?
- **Revenue**: Did they pay us?
- Use OKRs (Objectives and key results.)

WHEN AND HOW WOULD YOU EVOLVE YOUR METRICS OVER TIME?

Use diagnostics early on until you know that the direction you've chosen is the right one.

As certainty increases, evolve the metrics into short-term objectives and key results.

As the change comes to an end, reflect on all of the measurements used, how useful they were, and how you might change them for the next change.

At this point, the metrics should be more focused on outcomes, but even so, we tend to retrofit the metric to match the ROI we put in our business case. You need to decide if it's more important to play the business game or do something meaningful.

That last part is an important one. I mentioned that I am cynical of metrics, but sometimes it's essential that people feel good that the effort of the change was worth it.

Use your best judgement to balance diagnostics that help you course-correct versus measurements that justify the change's investment.

For me, this about making the invisible visible and giving people in organizations options for finding meaningful metrics.

Employee, customer, and stakeholder satisfaction are always my go-to measurements because they quantify it with a number (like an NPS score) and they also provoke discussion.

The worst thing that can happen is that we use our playbooks and scorecards as replacements for conversations.

HOW I REFRAME THE 7TH PRINCIPLE

Working software is the primary measure of progress.

FUZZY DIAGNOSTICS HELP us see progress, and give us the ability course-correct sooner.

HOW IT GUIDES MY ACTIONS

Debates have raged on for over a decade about how to measure the effectiveness of an agile coach. I always use a modified NPS:

- How likely would you recommend Jason as a coach?
- How valuable has it been having Jason as a coach?
- Why did you give the rating you did?

This tells me two things:

1. People see I'm here to help because I make my feedback public. If the rating is low because I'm not helpful, they can fire me, or I'll leave.
2. People see a different way to measure complex change, and it helps them find more meaningful metrics.

Here's an example:

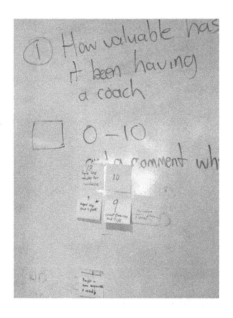

ADAPTING TO THE PACE

Agile processes promote sustainable development. The sponsors, developers, and users should be able to maintain a constant pace indefinitely.

* * *

WHAT IS THE ORGANIZATION'S NATURAL PACE OF CHANGE?

*A*ll organizations have a natural pace of change. Big organizations change slower than smaller ones, but they all have specific periods where dedicating time to change works better than other periods.

A great example is one organization I talked to, but didn't work with, who wanted to start an agile transformation in September.

That was a few weeks after they finalized their roadmap and budget for the year. This is a common pattern in larger organizations. August is the month for doing the annual plan for the following year, locking in budget, headcount, and aligning to HR objectives and performance management.

In their view, they ear-marked the money, had the plan, and now wanted to execute it in an agile way. Nicely, I told them it wouldn't work, and there's nothing they can do about because there is far too much organizational inertia:

- Performance mandates can't be changed.
- Stakeholder, board, and shareholder expectations are already set.
- Business objectives are defined and mapped to project outcomes.

Timing is everything. If they've already filled up 100% of the schedule for the next year, piling on a complex change that is mostly at odds with their current reality is going to stress everyone out.

In a different organization, mid-November to the end of December was their high season. No new features or business changes would happen because the holiday season was their most crucial revenue-generating season.

For them, that was a perfect time for training and changing things, so there was time for experimenting and learning.

You need to know the right intervention points, what typically triggers change, how change is accepted, and what the natural pace of change is for the organization.

WHAT DAY-TO-DAY WORK IS COMPETING WITH THE CHANGE?

Again, this is usually due to a lack of cohesion. For example, early in my change career, I would take my orders to do the change, and parachute into a team that wasn't ready.

In many cases, the teams have deadlines that need their focus. Moving to a pull-based approach in a situation where there are multiple teams works well. Teams that are ready can pull change, teams that aren't ready can delay.

WHO'S OVERLOADED WITH WORK?

This contradicts my previous point, but it's important to consider. I worked for my first startup in 2000. I'd pull an all-nighter once a week to get stuff deployed into production because it needed to be done.

As we grew, we hired more people, and quickly. A few of the other developers persuaded me to slow down so they could build a proper tool to automate something I had hacked together.

Eventually, I let go of my ego and listened.

Some people will always object to having their time taken away, and it's our responsibility to find the right balance between push and pull.

WHERE IS THE *PUSH* FOR THE CHANGE COMING FROM?

Speaking of push, who's asking for the change? Why are they asking for it and why do we, as change agents, feel that we have to push?

I grew up playing organized sports, so I developed a deep competitive spirit. There are times when I want to get something done just because I want to get it done.

This book is a great example. I wrote the whole thing inside of one-week and blocked out everything. I made a few tweaks during the copyediting, but the point was to get it done because I could wordsmith these pages forever.

You need to understand where the push is coming from and gain clarity around how important it is to go fast. Everyone has a boss, so the orders you have from your boss are likely trickling down from someone else. Ask:

- What would happen if we paused this change for now?
- Is there a less disruptive way to go about it?
- Should we increase the disruption to spring people into action?

HOW I REFRAME THE 8TH PRINCIPLE

Agile processes promote sustainable development. The sponsors, developers, and users should be able to maintain a constant pace indefinitely.

Apply agile to change gives me the ability to balance a push-and-pull approach to change so we can dedicate time to change when we're ready.

HOW IT GUIDES MY ACTIONS

- **Become enterprise aware:** Your eyes, ears, and brain are your most important allies. Walk around, and see how tired, or energized, people are.
- **Look for intervention spots:** I take time to understand the organization's existing rituals and rhythms to help my clients explore options that balance the push and pull of change. It's likely you can get people's time by piggybacking on an existing ritual.
- **Pull-based approach**: I mentioned this story in *Lean Change Management*. One of the consultants we worked with started using change Kanban boards that allowed teams to pull change when ready. If a team were up against a hard deadline, we'd leave them alone. If they were in a lull, we'd spend more time with them. While

it's hard to quantify, this reduced stress with people in the team because they could focus on delivery, not the change. When they was more time, they could focus on the change. The schedule was pull-based and based on demand, not pushed based on a forward-looking plan.

ADAPTABLE CHANGE PROCESS

Continuous attention to technical excellence and good design enhances
agility.

* * *

AGILE VS AGILE: WHAT'S BEING DISCIPLINED, AND WHAT'S JUST CHANGING STUFF WHENEVER WE FEEL LIKE IT?

*I*t would be easy to adapt this principle to change by interpreting it as being about best practice.

We could design a magnificent process on paper that fails miserably in the real world, much like an architect can over-engineer a solution that looks great in a diagram.

This one is tough. We all want to believe we're the most competent change agent, but for me, this principle is more about matching the approach to the environment.

A great example is the *digital factory* model that every bank, insurance company, and telecom implemented around 2014. Most of us older agile coaches knew this in the early 2000s, but there was no way they were going to listen until they learned why they should try it.

I worked with an organization that emailed requirements back and forth. It would be impossible for them to leap to an advanced practice called behaviour-driven development until they learned a more basic practice, like user stories, first.

By contrast, in another organization, they were well past user stories, but professed to be new to agile. Their maturity level told me they didn't need something so basic, and it was ok to start with something more advanced.

In change, it's the same. If people in different departments won't even talk to each other, telling them they need to change their mindset probably isn't going to work.

Meet them where they're at, and agree on one small step forward.

WHAT'S THE CHANGE EQUIVALENT OF *TECHNICAL EXCELLENCE* AND *GOOD DESIGN*?

This one is tough, and it's less about the practices for me. In software, technical excellence and good design help us safely change our software quickly.

In change, we're dealing with cognition. That means how people understand the purpose of the change, the direction we're going, and how we're getting there. That's harder to change compared to software.

For me, this becomes more of an attitude of having short feedback loops that help us reflect on the change, and the approach we're taking to implement the change.

HOW DO YOU KNOW IF YOU HAVE ACHIEVED THE CHANGE EQUIVALENT OF TECHNICAL EXCELLENCE AND GOOD DESIGN?

Again, this is much easier in software. If a stakeholder wants to add a field to a page and the team comes back with a guess of six months, the design is probably terrible.

In software, you have automated tests and builds that give you immediate feedback on your solution's state. In change, a good indication is the number of groans about having to follow processes that don't help.

Another great indicator is the number of times a stakeholder or team member wants to change something about the change and the process gets in the way.

Suppose you're following the Scrum framework which is time-boxed to two-week sprints. Imagine something radically changes on the first day of the sprint, would you wait until the sprint was over because you already committed to a chunk of work?

* * *

HOW I REFRAME THE 9TH PRINCIPLE FOR CHANGE

Continuous attention to technical excellence and good design enhances agility.

A WELL-DESIGNED change process gives us the ability to help and support people without getting in the way for the sake of having standardized practices.

* * *

A SHORT STORY ABOUT HOW IT GUIDES MY ACTIONS

I was working with an organization that had an unbelievably complicated process for onboarding agile teams.

Step 1: Initial conversation with Biff. Biff comes in with his clipboard and asks a bunch of generic Scrum-based questions like:

- Do you have a team space?
- Do you have a 100% dedicated team?

- Do you have a 100% product owner?

Step 2: Biff hands you off to Sally, who onboards your team to the mandated agile project management lifecycle tool.

Step 3: Sally hands you off to Joe, who puts you through the standardized agile process training.

I'm stopping here to be polite. Yes, it was that bad. When our team talked to them, we didn't get past Step 1 because we were working on a big, global HR project that had 11 SMEs and no single product owner.

We were told we weren't *authorized* to run an agile project.

So we detached from the centralized COE, and I came up with a *zero to ready to start in 3 days* process for our division which included:

1) A 30-minute conversation with the highest stakeholder on the business and IT sides

2) A team liftoff including:

- Alignment on purpose with most senior stakeholders
- General introduction to agile
- General introduction to flow-based versus time-based agile methods
- Team working agreements
- Story map and backlog representing the first X months of work (depending on the project)

3) Followup retrospective with everyone in one month

We moved away from the authoritarian playbook used by the COE, and towards a fit-for-purpose strategy with foundations in the agile manifesto.

This is good design and technical excellence, in my view. The liftoff process was abstracted enough, so teams were free to choose their path based on what they needed. The liftoff process I designed abstracted the context so it didn't matter if it was a three month project with one team, or three year program with twenty teams, we would agree on the least amount of process, working agreements, and a commitment to changing when we needed to change. That's adaptability.

As I used this process more and more, a pattern became clear. More highly regulated programs and projects naturally had more restrictive processes. Less regulated and experimental projects had essentially no process, except a loose agreement to validate assumptions any way possible.

The fact that we agreed on the approach together, within the context of any organizational constraints is what made it work.

KEEP IT SIMPLE

Simplicity — the art of maximizing the amount of work not done — is essential.

* * *

HOW DO YOU SAY NO TO STAKEHOLDERS WHO WANT YOU TO PUSH MORE CHANGE WHEN YOU KNOW THE TIME ISN'T RIGHT?

From my experience, stakeholders push because their vision of what the reality should be doesn't match what they see.

They might not *see* enough progress, which might lead them to believe the change team isn't doing anything or being too passive.

This is a perfect opportunity to switch the conversation towards prioritization. If you don't think the timing is right, give them evidence that people aren't ready, or that there are more important things to work on.

Visualization helps a lot here. It's hard to justify the feeling that teams are overworked or overburdened with change so if you can somehow visualize what's in progress, you can choose to prioritize the day-to-day with the change work.

HOW DO YOU PRIORITIZE CHANGE WORK?

I've asked this question hundreds of times in my workshops. How do you know what you should be working on?

It sounds like a dumb question, but when change agents think about it, most of the time it comes down to gut feel.

Yes, there is a plan in place, and activities or experiments happening, but the right thing to do is almost always based on feel.

Do you have a way to prioritize change work? There are plenty of ways agile delivery teams do this using old techniques like Kano surveys, MoSCoW (Must, Should, Could, Won't), and new techniques like theme scoring for users' stories.

HOW MUCH COMPLEXITY DO YOU ADD TO YOUR CHANGE OR CHANGE PROCESS DUE TO UNTESTED OR UNVALIDATED ASSUMPTIONS?

I ask myself, *"am I (or are we) adding or changing process for process sake, or is it actually valuable?"* I talked to a large organization that was looking to develop a new change framework. The goal was to do enough research to create an all-encompassing framework that everyone would adhere to. I've seen countless large organizations do the same thing.

Get a couple of people to spend months evaluating methods, in theory, building PowerPoints, playbooks and best practices and then wonder why their change agents have lost the ability to think in the moment.

I'm not saying it's valuable to have *something*, I'm saying the more complicated you make your change process, the less likely people will think about what they're doing.

HOW DO YOU MINIMIZE YOUR CHANGE PROCESS SO YOU CAN FOCUS ON PEOPLE?

Minimum viable change process. There's a nice catch phrase for you! In all seriousness, change is much more of an art than a science. The attitude, personality, and temperament you have as a change agent is the most important factor.

If you value structure and control, you're more likely to see change through a process lens and miss the essential people stuff. If you value collaboration and people, you're more likely to see change through a people-first approach and miss essential structures.

Much like I advocate for co-creation of change, I advocate for co-creation of the approach to change by the change team.

* * *

HOW I REFRAME THE 10TH PRINCIPLE

> Simplicity — the art of maximizing the amount of work not done — is essential.

MINIMAL VIABLE CHANGE PROCESS. Don't let the process get in the way of minding the people.

* * *

A STORY ABOUT HOW IT GUIDES MY ACTIONS

I have a bad habit of getting bored quickly. Sometimes when working on longer contracts, or as an employee, I'd want to change things just for the sake of change.

While working at The Commission, the organization I mentioned in *Lean Change Management*, I was bored with our daily stand-ups. It didn't seem like they were still valuable for people based on the energy I thought I was seeing.

Keeping it simple, I posted a satisfaction flip-chart asking people to mark a point on the chart that defined how useful they thought the standup was from 0, not at all valuable, to 10, super valuable.

It turns out it was all in my mind. People still liked it, so instead of changing the process, I let it go and moved on.

On another occasion, we were synchronizing our gigantic physical Kanban board with an electronic tool and creating complicated lists and spreadsheets to track risks.

We did this because the external consultants did it before our department was created. Since I'm the laziest person on the planet, I wanted to see if I needed to do it at all, so, I ran an experiment.

Instead of sending the link to the tool, spreadsheet, and list in our update email, I just sent a link to the online tool and a spreadsheet on our intranet site. I was tracking the link to see how many people clicked through.

Turns out less than 1% of people looked at it, and there was no governance rule in place that said we needed all this complexity. After two weeks running this experiment, we stopped updating the tool and spreadsheets. We proclaimed the physical board as a single source of truth. Simple, and easy.

THE PEOPLE WHO WRITE THE PLAN
DON'T FIGHT THE PLAN

The best architectures, requirements, and designs emerge from self-organizing teams.

* * *

WHAT'S THE CHANGE EQUIVALENT OF ARCHITECTURE, REQUIREMENTS, AND DESIGN?

I relate this principle to the *adaptable change* chapter. In organizations that have an agile coaching, change, OD, Communications, Process Improvement, and HR teams, it's easy for them to suffer from lack of cohesion.

Generally speaking, agile coaches are more likely to be loose and go with the flow compared to communications people who might be more rigid and structured. Obviously that's not a truism, but just know that each group has their own distinct view of how change should happen.

Instead of working against each other, design an approach for change together. I worked with one large organization where we did just that. These groups worked together on a variety of changes, all in the context of a generational transformation. That means, they didn't see their transformation as a one-year project, they saw it as the next decade of evolution for their organization.

When it came time to plan the annual summit[1], me, the agile coaches, change consultants, HR, and comms people all worked together to create it.

We relied on the diversity of perspective to create our approach versus following a method, framework, or playbook.

WHICH TEAMS ARE SELF-ORGANIZING? THE CHANGE TEAM? THE PEOPLE AFFECTED BY THE CHANGE?

As a change agent, I work extremely hard to bring the organization's perspective of the change to the people affected so they can figure out how to accomplish it together.

The change teams I work with create their working agreements, including their team's vision, how they'll organize the work, how and when they'll meet, and all of the good stuff that is discussed during team liftoffs.

Early on in change, hosting open spaces[2] and lean coffee sessions[3] are perfect for making the most of self-organizing teams. It helps you figure out what topics are the most important for people and they'll likely give you a bunch of better ideas you might not have thought about.

WHAT GUARDRAILS ARE IN PLACE TO PROTECT SELF-ORGANIZATION FROM SLIPPING INTO CHAOS?

On one extreme, self-organizing with no constraints is chaotic. E.g. While working as a product owner in an organization, there was no IT budget in place, and the CEO wanted redundancy and failover capabilities for our SaaS solution. The CTO and architect built a monstrosity of an infrastructure that almost bankrupted the company.

On the other extreme, too many constraints don't allow for creative thinking. E.g. In a large financial organization, the Agile COE had decided that all teams would use Scrum. When the department I was working on started using Kanban, they told us that it wasn't a supported method, and we weren't *allowed* to use it.

As Jerry Weinberg once told me, you don't know what the line is until you cross it. When it comes to putting the right guardrails in place, the key is knowing how leaders will react when the line gets crossed.

As I mentioned earlier, the *reaction* to the problem becomes the problem.

* * *

HOW I REFRAME THE 11TH PRINCIPLE

The best architectures, requirements, and designs emerge from self-organizing teams.

INVITE PEOPLE TO THE PARTY, ask them to dance, and give them the option to opt-out

* * *

A STORY ABOUT HOW IT GUIDES MY ACTIONS

There's a right time and a wrong time for co-creation. While I did write this book in the summer of 2019, I re-wrote this part in August 2020 because of COVID-19. You've probably noticed that I am flipping between simple advice via bullet points to longer stories in these last few chapters.

We're a week away from going back to school, and my kids' high school has 2500 students. In my home province of Ontario, there are over two million students enrolled in public elementary and high schools. That means there are close to four-million parents, guardians, or caretakers who have better ideas for how the government should approach safely opening schools. Add in the 130,000 teachers, and roughly 7,500 school administrators, and you've got a massively complex change on your hands.

From a change perspective, more constraints make sense here. While our school board is great at taking input and revising as necessary, they are going to decide how to do it and that's probably best. It's hard enough to get five people at a party to agree on toppings, there's zero chance the school board will figure out how to coalesce four million or so people on a back-to-school plan.

This is my long-winded way of saying my approach is to give people a choice. I've been running my own businesses since the early 2000s, and believe me; there are days when I would love for someone else to do the thinking for me. I'd love to execute a bunch of tasks by following whatever the coach or consultant tells me. At the end of the day, it's more satisfying sense of responsibility knowing things that go well, or not well, are because of choices I consciously made.

Getting back to doing change in a non-software environment, many years back, I ran a one-day version of my workshop at a conference. We spent the more than an hour hour just getting people to self-organize into teams! You can read a more detailed account of this story on my blog4 , but why it took so long came down to two main things:

1. The people thought it was MY workshop and I was supposed to TELL THEM how to learn and what to do.
2. There was a low bias towards action from people in the room.

After they finally self-organized into teams, one person said, *"You know, we always say people won't do anything until we tell them, but that's exactly what we did to you!"*

The lesson: Sometimes you need to provoke people into action, sometimes you need to let them organize on their own, and other times, you give them the tasks to execute.

The key is, the people affected by the change should have the choice, so give it to them.

INSPECT AND ADAPT

*At regular intervals, the team reflects on how to become more effective,
then tunes and adjusts its behaviour accordingly.*

* * *

HOW OFTEN DOES YOUR CHANGE TEAM REFLECT AND TUNE YOUR CHANGE PROCESS?

This one is difficult in larger organizations where adherence to the process is more important. That isn't necessarily a bad thing. I once worked with an HR team where the VP said that agile would never work for him. As I picked away at the statement, he said that it's better if he screws up payroll for 80,000 people by following the process rather than taking the risk of trying something new.

Fair enough. I'd probably have the same attitude in his position.

Most of the change teams I've worked with do all of the change process definition upfront, get sign-off from leaders, build playbooks, intranet sites, manuals, do training, and more.

I'm not saying some of that *isn't* valuable, but it does create a sense of having to follow the process because so much time money was invested in bringing it to life.

Then, when any problem arises, the first question is always, *"Did you follow <process X?>"*

One of the best change teams I've worked with is based in a large insurance company, and they have a fit-for-purpose approach to change. That is, they have so many different pieces to pick from. It sounds like a playbook, but it's not.

For example, when uncertainty is extremely high, like when they want to create an innovation program, they use the *go talk to them* process.

The onus is on the change agent to know how to have a well-facilitated conversation versus walking in with a clipboard and a list of talking points from a playbook.

I use this technique with agile teams. It's called a *satisfaction-o-gram* and I , have the team list all the practices they do and rate how effective they are from 0 to 10. Then, we choose an area of focus, dig deeper, and figure out how to magnify the good or fix the bad.

You can do the same thing with your change team on a quarterly or semi-annual basis.

HOW ARE STAKEHOLDERS INVOLVED?

I am a fan of inviting stakeholders into any ceremonies, such as planning, stand-ups, and retrospectives. I will guarantee you that no stakeholders are looking at your pillars, change diagrams, and other artifacts. Unless they used to be a change agent, in which case, they might just want to show you how much they know.

This isn't only an exercise on refining the approach to change, it also gives stakeholders a window into your thought process so they'll understand how you and your team make decisions.

Another benefit is that if you are using agile practices like visualizing your work, using stand-ups, or doing creative retrospectives, they might bring those practices to other areas of the organization, or better yet, to the executive team.

Again, much like co-creation with the people affected by the change, give them a choice, and let them opt-out.

WHAT ABOUT PEOPLE AFFECTED BY THE CHANGE?

While working in a large telecom, we were coming up on our six-month anniversary of starting an agile transformation. Twenty-five teams were practicing agile, and we ran monthly retrospectives that all teams were allowed to join.

This is how we decided what the right experiments were in the context of the organizational strategy canvas[1].

For the six-month anniversary, we did a massive asynchronous retrospective that took just over a week that answered the ultimate question: It's been six months that we've been trying agile, should we keep going?

The answer was yes. That led to a new chapter, where we took inventory of what we did, what happened, and what we could do next.

Not only did that change what experiments we did, but it also changed how we approached the change.

HOW I REFRAME THE 12TH PRINCIPLE FOR CHANGE

At regular intervals, the team reflects on how to become more effective, then tunes and adjusts its behaviour accordingly.

TAKE the time to stop and understand how people feel about the change, think about how you can change the change, and how you approach the change

* * *

A SHORT STORY...OR TWO

In January of 2012, my team won a lean startup weekend contest[2]. Until then, I was doing and coaching teams on retrospectives, but lean startup added another dimension to my thinking. The key point they hammered home was to go talk to customers. In change, that means getting out from behind closed doors and seeing first hand what help and support people need before executing on your assumptions.

We assume our approach for change is correct. We assume we know the most and know the best way to do it. We're all biased in some way, and I'm heavily biased towards giving people a choice.

I default to a facilitation and coaching stance, and sometimes that isn't the right approach. In one large financial organization, that approach didn't work because it was too incompatible with how change worked.

I had to push more, which I always felt was wrong, but by retrospecting frequently, I got feedback that helped me modify my approach.

One of my favourite learning opportunities was working with Andrew Annett on a manager retrospective. He started by writing one simple question on the board:

"what are you tolerating?"

Instead of doing a typical retrospective, the goal was to have an exploration session with what the managers felt they *had* to do just because we coaches were there.

It was probably one of the best discussions I've ever had. It was so honest and raw.

While I did mention retrospectives help you reflect on the change, and how you're doing the change, it's also such an essential ceremony to stop and talk with people without feeling you have to improve something just because the process says you're supposed to.

HOW IT GUIDES MY ACTIONS

Finding balance: Too much feedback and reflection can lead to decision paralysis. The concept of *inspect and adapt* is as old as humankind. While attributed to Deming, the PDCA (Plan-Do-Check-Act) cycle, or Shewhart cycle, is all you need. Lean Startup reduced that idea to the three-step Build-Measure-Learn cycle, and I'll further reduce it to a two-step cycle: Act-Reflect!

PART IV - CHANGING YOUR VIEW OF CHANGE

"You can change yourself and you can change the situation but you absolutely cannot change other people. Only they can do that." - Joanna Trollope

* * *

In the opening chapter I mentioned three things most people consider when they are wanting to be *more agile* in change management:

- Transforming how you manage change work
- Transforming how you think about change
- Transforming how you work with agile teams

I've been a product owner, Scrum master, and team member on agile teams. I've been an external and internal agile coach, and

I've worked as an organizational change agent on business process change and organizational change.

Out of all of those experiences, being a product owner had the most profound effect on how I view change.

I see the *change* as a *product*, and the *people affected by the change* as *end users*. That definitely sounds weird, considering my view on putting people first!

What I mean is, when I worked as a product owner, I learned much faster by going to client offices and working on product discovery with them. That was the best way to test my assumptions about the product.

Seeing first hand what our clients life at work was like was instrumental in figuring out the best way to evolve existing and to create new products.

And before that, my experience working as a technical support agent at a global call centre set me down the path of being a helper.

That was the long-winded way of me saying that I have always viewed change as a service function. That is, I am here to serve the people and the organization. That doesn't mean I do whatever they want, it means I must help them discover what the right change is, how to go about it, and leave as much of my biases out as I can.

It has been extremely difficult for me to work in some enterprise organizations that see change as a set of structured, and standardized practices and steps. While I do understand why they want gigantic, all-encompassing frameworks, it's far too constraining and frustrating and it just doesn't work.

If you're new to *agile change*, or agile in general, it's probably going to be hard to see change differently. In these final chapters, I'll move away from asking you questions, and more toward offering advice that I hope you find valuable to build a bridge between what you already know, and what *making change more agile* might look like for you.

TRANSFORMING HOW YOU MANAGE CHANGE WORK

his one is easiest of all three. Agile practices have been around for decades. While the agile manifesto was created in 2001, that doesn't mean no one collaborated in a meaningful way before that. I've always said everything in the agile ecosystem has already been created, which is true if you look deep enough. The manifesto took timeless ideas and organized the words differently making them more accessible to the masses.

I like to think of this section as the foundational set of ideas that are an absolute must. If you're unable to implement these simple, effective practices in your organization, the other two are going to be much more challenging.

- **Visualize your work**. While it's harder to physically visualize work with sticky notes and whiteboards in a post-COVID world, the goal is to make decisions about the work by seeing the work, and to have a single source of truth

- **Decide on time-boxed vs flow-based process**: Time-box = applying Scrum, Flow-based = applying Kanban. Even better, use both. Scrumban or Kanban-um if you need a label, but flow work based on value, and keep a regular cadence of important ceremonies
- **Commit to retrospectives** no matter which process you use.
- **Have a daily standup** and invite stakeholders.

The most straightforward process frees up your brain to think about more complex things, and it helps you focus on the people-side of change.

VISUALIZE YOUR WORK

Here's an example of an agile transformation wall I used in a large bank:

Remember, agile people aren't pro-visualization and anti-tool out of some anarchist view. It's harder to manage the work when we can't see it. Visualizing work leads to better conversations and decision making.

While it may seem like extra work, the purpose of visualizing work is different. It's not designed to replace documents, or wikis that hold more details. I'll walk you through the examples of the agile transformation walls from the bank:

The first image shows the coordination of multiple changes the leadership team was working on via swim-lanes:

- People and culture programs being run by HR
- 'Agile stuff' being orchestrated by me
- Process improvement program
- Technical and architecture programs/projects

Beside that was the program Kanban wall with all of the high-level programs that were happening. (I can't show you the exact program visual because of privacy, but don't worry, there will be plenty of examples at changewayfinder.com you can check out!)

The second image shows the details about the agile transformation including:

- Purpose of the visualization: So people know what they're looking at
- Major programs, or themes: Each of these included the purpose, and who's working on it.
- Status update (*How's it going?* Column): The big coloured stickies (shown below) with a date and note. Red = blocked, Green = good

Here's a closer picture of the status update section:

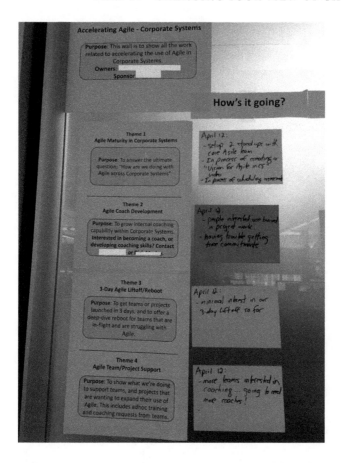

How this helped:

- It removed complicated status reports because they weren't necessary.
- It showed people that change was happening. Some people would ask me about it, others didn't care.
- It held me accountable and showed that I use the techniques I'm asking other people to use.

Finally, here are a couple of close up pictures showing a few ideas for visualizing lower-level details:

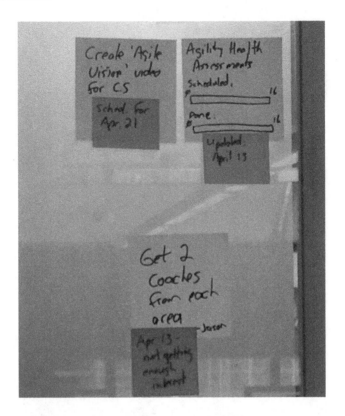

Blue sticky notes: Last updated, and scheduling information.

Red sticky notes: A blocker with details about why it's blocked.

Progress indicators: We were mandated to use the Agility Health radar tool, which I think is pretty cool, if used correctly. This showed that out of 16 teams, no one used it yet, and nothing was scheduled. That probably seems odd, but the sticky note was placed in the *In progress* column because I was doing some exploratory work.

DECIDE ON TIME-BOXED, OR FLOW...OR BOTH!

Scrum is a time-boxed process that helps you get in a rhythm. The challenge with only using Scrum to manage change work is figuring out what the *potentially shippable product* would be at the end of the sprint. This is easy in software, hard in change.

Kanban allows you to focus on value first and pull more work as you complete work.

I always use both because:

With Scrum: I like rhythms, and to make use of the time-boxed ceremonies like sprint planning, daily stand-ups, sprint reviews, and retrospectives.

With Kanban: I don't get locked into committing to two-weeks of change work like Scrum states, but instead, flow work and use the book-ends of the Scrum ceremonies to see how things are progressing.

COMMIT TO RETROSPECTIVES

This is by far the most important agile practice to use. Whatever process flow you pick, use the retrospectives to reflect on what is, and isn't working and change it.

I highly recommend RetroMat[1] to find a bunch of awesome techniques, as well as Esther Derby's Agile Retrospectives book[2].

CONDUCT DAILY STANDUPS

Meet in front of your visualization, whether it's in-person or virtually, and invite outside groups such as the PMO, audit/compliance, HR, or any group who needs to be aware of what's going on.

There's a difference between a Scrum stand-up and a Kanban stand-up:

Scrum: 3 questions are asked: what did you work on yesterday, what will you work on today, and what is blocking you?

Kanban: Starting from the column directly to the left of *done*, you discuss what it'll take to complete what's in that column to enable flow.

I told this story in my last book, so apologies if it's a repeat for you! At The Commission, the company in the book, we invited the business PMO to our enterprise stand-ups and they documented whatever they needed to. We didn't try to change them, we merely provided a simpler way for them to see what was happening with IT-related work.

MINIMUM VIABLE CHANGE PROCESS

These basic techniques are mostly known in today's world. Back when I started visualizing work in the early 2000s, people thought I was crazy. I'd like to say it's because I wanted to be more innovative in managing work, but in reality it was because I was super-lazy and wanted to free my brain up to focus on important work instead of trying to get that damn Excel sheet formatted properly.

HOW TO CHALLENGE YOURSELF AND YOUR ORGANIZATION:

I mentioned that the argument against using big visible walls is that people who are used to big project schedules and documents see this as a duplication of work.

What they don't understand is that the detail on your big visible walls should be minimal. It's designed to store just enough details to have a conversation that allows for quick decision-making. It's not designed to replace more detailed documents. Although, in my opinion, you should always question the need of these documents, but that's a discussion for another day!

Another argument against it, especially in a post-COVID world, is that we can't do a big visual wall if we're all remote . There are tools to make it easier, but remember, the intent of the visible wall is two-fold:

- To be a single source of truth.
- To encourage meaningful conversations that help us make better decisions.

There are always some type of project management activities that need to happen. Some are valuable, and some are simply habits that we do, but don't know why.

A good practice to challenge yourself and your organization is to audit your process and artefacts:

- How useful is *<this process>* for *us* from 0 to 10, and why?
- Ask stakeholders how useful this process/artefact is for *them* from 0 to 10, and why.
- Talk to the PMO or governance people and find out what they need (odds are it's just your boss that wants to cover their ass.)

Don't disrupt things just to be disruptive. If you are highly regulated and you get frequently audited, do what's necessary to manage that, but at least challenge it!

TRANSFORMING HOW YOU THINK ABOUT CHANGE

A friend of mine once said that the only people resistant to change are change managers!

I'd agree with that. I'm tied to the practices I like, we all are. We're all biased towards our view of what we believe works. No process, method, playbook, or framework will change that unless we accept that it's our attitude and experiences that are primarily responsible for how we see change.

These are the rules I live by, and questions I ask of myself, because I am a highly competitive person and a self-professed control freak. I get so focused on the goal sometimes, I can lose sight of my own behaviours. By the way, declaring what you believe your biases are is a great practice for integrating with a new organization, or team. I always tell clients that I love the energy that change brings and that I can get bullish sometimes, but the intent is to make things better even though sometimes I come off as being abrasive.

- **What is it about my behaviour and approach that could be causing what I'm observing?** E.g. If I believe people are resisting change, what is it about my approach that might be a factor?
- **Do I want to win because I want to win, or am I pushing in the best interest of the organization?** I had a bad habit of assuming organizations that wanted to be more agile wanted to be more agile. I'd push, and push, and then I realized they wanted help becoming clear about problems, and help with solving them. Understand what you're being asked to do.
- **Am I being congruent?** E.g. We all have a breaking point and we'll only compromise our values so far. If I feel I'm not being congruent, I check out.
- **Am I the right change agent?** E.g. I won't work with banks, insurance, telecoms, or any enterprise that doesn't align with my values. This isn't a knock against them, or my friends who work there. This is simply my choice of wanting to focus my energy elsewhere. That said, *transactional work* is ok. Transactional work is training where I will train them on agile and modern change practices, but I won't consult or coach them directly.
- **Who in the agile and change community do I completely agree with?** Whoever they are, stop reading and following them! Ok, that probably sounds weird because some of you probably agree with my writings. The point is, don't blindly follow someone because you already agree with them. Seek out people who respectfully challenge your beliefs.

- **Try it out**. Some of the ideas in this book might be scary. Declare your intent to experiment with your stakeholders so they understand why you're going to do what you're about to do. Courage of conviction will take you places.

Most importantly, for me, trying to look at change from different perspectives is what helped me enjoy the work more. What helped me realize this was the pattern of seeing so many change agents I've worked with over the years leave organizations that were making them miserable.

When I enjoyed the work more, I was more likely to help others enjoy their work more. That sounds corny, but it's true.

I suppose you could say this chapter is about changing *your* behaviour as a change agent, instead of focusing on getting other people to change *their* behaviour.

After traveling the world since 2014 and finding patterns, five universals patterns stood out that helped change agents see change differently. We're used the traditional view of what good change management is:

- **Create urgency:** This includes the god-awful horrible phrase, "creating a burning platform." For the love of the universe, please stop using that. The phrase's origin is literally about a burning platform on an oil rig where people either jump or die.
- **Get buy-in:** This means we've decided on the change,

have the perfect plan, and now we need to get people on-board.

- **Communicate**: This usually manifests itself in broadcasting techniques, like newsletters, town-halls with scripted questions, and intranet sites, or posters hung on the walls.
- **Execution**: Manage the schedule and execute the tasks.
- **Mitigate resistance**: Have a plan in place to deal with those pesky humans who resist change.

I discovered that those five *things* are important, but we can look at each of them differently. I decided to call them the Five Universals of Change[1] and it's not about either-or, it's about balance when to use which approach.

Co-creation over getting buy-in: You'll focus on diversity of thought and inclusion. This means invite people to the party, ask them to dance, but let them opt-out instead of doing your best sales pitch to get them on-board.

Meaningful dialogue over broadcasting: You'll use lean coffee and other dialogue-encouraging practices to uncover what people need and want instead of broadcasting comms plans at people

Cause & purpose or creating urgency: You'll rally people around a common purpose, knowing that not everyone will want to come along instead of trying to in-still urgency in people by coercing or bullying them.

Experimentation over executing tasks: You'll realize that some-times the goal is to learn, not execute tasks and foster a safe-to-learn culture, which is a positive spin on the mediocrity-inducing safe-to-fail statement.

Response to change over resistance to change: You'll realize that what you label resistance is the natural response people have to change. That's the data you need to shape your change differently instead of blaming every failure on resistance or lack of buy-in.

These Five Universals aren't about this is right, that is wrong. It's about knowing how to balance them by stepping outside of your beliefs and looking at the context through different lenses.

You'll find more details about these Five Universals on the Change Wayfinder, but the next book that explores it in much more detail is already in progress!

Briefly, it's about changing your view of change, and choosing the pieces that fit best in your context.

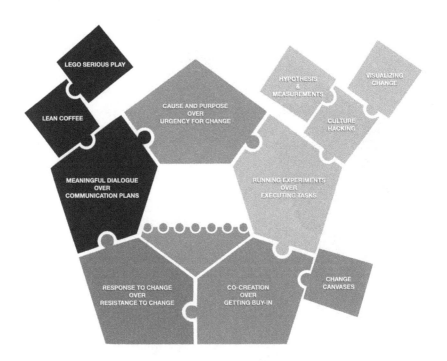

Changing the lens by which you look at change requires you to use the most important tools you have: *Your eyes, ears, and brain.* Thanks to my friends and colleagues Ro Gorell and Charlotte Mawle for that one!

TRANSFORMING HOW YOU INTEGRATE WITH AGILE TEAMS

*T*ransforming how you integrate with agile teams is reasonably simple and similar to the first point about transforming how you manage change work. The difference is, you control how you manage change work. Integrating with agile teams requires you to align to how they do work, which might mean you need to change how you manage change work in some way.

First, some pre-cursors:

- **Flip the bit** from seeing what you do as a change agent from control to a service function. The agile team is directly delivering value, you are supporting them to do that, not coercing them into following your lead.
- **Consider yourself an air traffic controller** so you can visualize the moving parts of agile programs and link

up activities from the agile teams to what your organization needs.

- **Integrate and visualize** your change work into the agile team's workflow. (E.g. Ask the team if you can attend their planning, sprint reviews, and standup as an observer.)
- **Sit with the team** if there is a substantial business change. (E.g. If the agile team is replacing a system that requires 10,000 people to be re-trained, you must be involved daily.)
- **Don't impose your view and process** on the agile team. Adapt and integrate your change process into theirs.
- **You are the bridge and connector** between the agile team and the greater organization. Your biggest friends are the Scrum masters and agile coaches. Work with them, not against them.

There will be overlap with your role as a change manager and the Scrum master, agile coach, managers, project, and program managers. Each may report up through different hierarchies so there may be quite a bit of complexity, duplication of documentation and process.

In the *Transforming How You Manage Change Work* chapter, I suggested you audit your own processes and artefacts to see what is, and isn't useful. Do the same thing here, but with all of the supporting functions involved with the agile team.

WHAT TO EXPECT

Agile coaches can get very defensive when an outsider tries to intervene in how they are working. Actually, I should say inexperienced agile coaches can get very defensive. Back in 2015, I was in Melbourne running a bunch of workshops and as luck would have it, there was an agile meetup and a change management meetup on two consecutive nights.

I was asked to speak at both about *agile change management* and the pattern was interesting:

Agile meetup: *"Those damn change people, trying to come in and step all over our team, imposing their views of how we must work. THEY. DON'T. GET. IT."*

Change meetup: *"Those damn agile coaches, disrupting the entire organization, and being clueless about how they effect the greater organization. THEY. DON'T. GET. IT"*

The agile meetup was first, so knowing I'd be two-doors down the next night at the change meetup, I asked a bunch of agile coaches to crash the party.

Long-story short, the version of agile the change managers were being introduced to were structured, standardized practices from big consulting firms. That made them believe agile was just another set of standards they had to follow. One change manager said that because they were doing *agile change management*, they had to write all of their documents in user story format: As a change manager, I want <whatever> so I can <get a result>.

The conversation was fantastic, and both camps agreed they were after the same results, but they hadn't considered what the other camp needed.

This has been my mission since 2014. Connect the change, agile, OD, and HR communities because we all want the same thing, we just forget to talk to each other sometimes.

BE A USEFUL ENGINE!

Be a helpful person and a link to all of the organizational stuff that typically gets ignored. You must help the agile team understand how they intersect with the rest of the organization because it might seem like they don't care when they might not be aware of the ripples they're creating.

You may be disappointed that there is no process diagram for how to do this. From my experience, a conversation with the agile team is the best place to start and these are the points that matter most:

Understand their context: What space is the agile delivery team in? Who are their customers? What is their release schedule like? What is the impact to the organization? (E. g. - are there substantial business processes changing? Is substantial training required? How are marketing and sales, and other teams impacted by what they're producing? Are there customer support implications?) - You can see how this can get complicated quickly.

Understand their processes: When do they host sprint reviews, stakeholder demos, customer showcases, focus group sessions etc.? Align your efforts with those rhythms.

Be clear about what you need: Much like you need to understand their content and processes, they need to understand the organizational impacts. The difference is that agile processes are pull-based and what gets delivered is based on the team's pace. While it's natural for the business to push, you must be the bridge and voice of reason between business and IT, especially if there is a hard separation between the two.

Educate the organization: Staple yourself to the agile coach, if the team has one, and educate the organization on the importance of tighter integration between the business and IT. At one organization, our coaching team called this our *outreach program.* We inspired HR, learning and development, executive teams and more to show them how to simply and coordinate better. The key point, it was their choice. We made them aware of what we could do, and they pulled us in when they needed and wanted to.

This is one way to educate the organization about how interconnected everything is:

This gigantic, shockingly ugly, Kanban board shows every idea and piece of work being stored in this organization's collective brain.

- **The far-left section:** Our principles, purpose of this visualization, and who our customers are.
- **The green grid:** A pull-based roadmap of ideas, not commitments. The swimlanes align to revenue streams and major product areas. The columns are, from left to right: Q3 2014 | Q2 2014 | Q1 2014 | This Quarter. The yellow sticky notes in the *This Quarter* column have small, coloured stickies on them. Those sticky notes show the teams who need to work on that stuff.
- **The middle section:** Mid-level detail such as epics, workflow diagrams and other mid-level details that came out of product discovery sessions.
- **The far-right:** Sprint details by team. That showed exactly what the teams were working on.

Here is a close-up of the far-left section:

On a different wall we visualized the history of the company:

This showed:

- A snapshot of the current state, number of customers, amount of data, etc.
- Timeline of major milestones and events such as when new customers came on board, when new products were released, awards, and major industry events.

I worked with Leandog and Jon Stahl on this. In his view, when you visit product companies who have physical products, you walk into their office and see what they do. When you visit software companies like this company, you see nothing and have no idea what they do.

Employees should feel proud of their accomplishments and this wall was in the front lobby so everyone saw it when they walked in, and so did customers.

Finally, these last two visualizations show the customer and data journeys through the organization and everything about their technology and tools:

WHY DOES THIS MATTER FOR CHANGE AGENTS?

Simple. It's about helping different areas of the organization understand each other's contexts. The top photo showed the customer and data flow through the organization and was used to troubleshoot problems and to help understand rough effort of making changes. The photo's ribbons show the flow of data and the far right yellow sticky notes show the physical screens the data shows up on.

The bottom photo exposed why there was confusion about features: too many systems tracked that stuff. In fact, this was the most technically competent organization I've worked in and they moved so fast that generating release notes was a problem.

Generating release notes is boring, but important to do. The technical teams always had more complicated work to do so I took that project over. I was their agile coach and since I used to be a developer, I helped automate a simple report that would be sent to anyone who wanted to see what was coming up in the next release, and what was just released.

Agile people often make fun of Jira. Jokes on them, this company used Jira and if they weren't using it, I wouldn't have been able to provide instant data to the business folks.

FINDING YOUR METAPHOR

Remember switchboard operators? I don't, but I know of them! They were the link between the caller and the call recipient. That's what change agents do, they act as a link between two groups, such as departments and people, management and employees, etc.

If that metaphor doesn't work for you, how about an air-traffic controller? They sit high-up and see how everything is interconnected with each other.

If that isn't a good metaphor, what about rally car navigators? The driver is focused on driving, the navigator is focused on helping them be aware of their surroundings and what is coming.

How you see your role as a change agent is the centrepiece of how you can best shift your thinking and approach for change.

PART V - WHAT'S CHANGE SINCE LEAN CHANGE MANAGEMENT?

The more things change, the more they stay the same. - Tom Keifer

* * *

Back in 2009 when I wrote the blog post that change everything for me, I didn't expect to embark on a worldwide quest to explore why some people were making change work, while others were getting stuck.

Today there are so many distractions with new acronyms, models, frameworks, loopy-looking diagrams, and step-by-step guides based on someone's opinion about how they see change.

Humans have a need to understand things. When I write or create diagrams and explainer videos, it's my way of conveying how I see the world of change. It's no more true than someone else's view, and when people ask me, *"How do I implement Lean Change Management?"* I struggle with how to respond.

The deeper I looked into answering that question, the more I found timeless and universal ideas that matter more than a new diagram or model.

A great example is how Alan Mulally approached the turn-around at Ford[1]. According to his interview with MIT, a weekly meeting was the centrepiece of his strategy.

He had the global department heads meet weekly and:

"Every week, we got together and went around the world. We looked at all the risks and opportunities and the business environments. We looked at our strategy. 'Does it still make sense? Are there any changes we need to make?' Then we looked at the details of our plan... You're constantly updating your sense of reality, but it's not just me doing it, it's the entire team."

I encourage you to read the full interview if you want to see how someone transcends the latest fashion with good ol', tried-and-true leadership capabilities.

Lean Change Management was about having the leanest, most simple change process possible that would allow change agents to focus on what matters versus following a process.

If your change process is lean and simple, it's more likely the change agents will think about how best to move change forward.

If your change process is bloated and complicated, it's more likely the change agents will follow the process as prescribed.

MODERN CHANGE MANAGEMENT

I'm sure some of you may have groaned at that phrase, and you may be thinking, *"Didn't you say earlier that we should stop and look around versus inventing something new?"*

Yes, yes I did. But these labels don't matter. I am only using them to give you a frame of how I think.

What became clear to me after traveling the world and connecting with so many change agents is that there were certain universal ideas that guided them toward facilitating more meaningful change. Those universal ideas were the five universals for change I mentioned in the *Transforming How You Think About Change* chapter.

Think of a good friend you have. Now think of when you met this person and how that friendship developed.

How did it happen?

Did you buy a playbook about how to cultivate a relationship? Did you follow a framework, method, or step-by-step process guide of best practices that would ensure successful friendship? What metrics did you put in place to measure the success and ensure the ROI of the time spent?

Of course not! That just sounds silly. The universal truths for establishing and maintaining a relationship with someone else is analogous to the universal truths for how meaningful change happens.

I discovered those truths by traveling the world and finding out what was important for change agents. I collected *change challenges* from hundreds of workshops and here is the categorized view of what change agents wanted to learn more about:

Some examples of the most common change challenges people had are:

- How can agile and change management be friends?
- How can I use more agile / lean tools in change?
- How can I get leaders / managers / stakeholders to buy into the change?
- How can I overcome change resistance?

This made me realize that agile change, lean change, modern change, and any other marketing label is just that, a label. This book is a great example, I called it *Change Agility* to bring attention to my ideas.

That is only the entry point, however. When you hear the term *agile*, or *agility*, your brain is already generating assumptions on what this book is about. If your brain told you it would be about how to apply a new process to be more agile in change, you'd probably hate this book. Although, you probably wouldn't have read this far, so it's a moot point!

Labels will come and go. Eventually people will get sick of agile change, lean change, modern change, and any other label, and move on to something else.

Larry Smith, an adjunct professor at the University of Waterloo said, *"When consultants start using the term, the idea is commoditized and in decline, and soon to be replaced with something else"*. This was at an *intrapreneur* conference, and he followed that up with, *"In 50 years, this conference will still be a thing, but it'll be called something different because these two foundational ideas will never change: competition and innovation. The more we innovate, the more competition we create. The more competition we create, the more we need to innovate."*

In the final chapters of Part V, I'll share a story about what happened with The Commission five years later. I'll also share a variety of agile change manifestos collected from various workshops around the world. These will show that it doesn't matter what country change agents are from or the size or industry of the organizations they serve, we all have the same challenges and we all share similar views of what being *more agile in change management* means.

WHAT HAPPENED WITH THE COMMISSION?

J kept in touch with folks at The Commission over the years because it's always nice to see how things evolve, especially because I spent a year of my life there. Every company I've visited and worked in has improved over time, but the 'failure' conversations seem to dominate social media because they're more fun to discuss.

As humans, we love drama. My friend, Andrew Annett, likes to say that our brains are like velcro when it comes to bad things, and like Teflon when it comes to good things. We remember the bad and always forget the good.

I'm not going to dig into the 70% failure myth in change management, or the Top 8 dysfunctions, or other nonsense, because it's all nonsense. No matter how small, organizational changes are far too complex to distill into a binary success or failure outcome.

I've had people ask me if the transformation at The Commission was a success, and I always answer it the same way:

When I left, things were better than when I started, and they continue to evolve.

It's easy for me to step in and see just how much progress has been made, so I sat down with a couple of people at The Commission in 2018 to hear more about what had changed. One of them said:

"If you would have written this book two years ago, we would have cried [telling you what happened since you left], but things are pretty good now, and getting better".

The Big Things

- CIO changes over the last six years.
- QMO team doesn't exist, and coaches and Scrum masters now sit in delivery streams.
- They still use Change Canvases when necessary.
- They always visualize work, albeit the gigantic enterprise Kanban board has become extinct (boards are all electronic now, focusing on projects and services.)
- The modernization program went live with the number of problems you could expect from a 3-year modernization program designed to move off mainframe technology and onto a modern tech stack. Some still blame 'agile' for all their problems related to this modernization.
- Change Management is no longer an afterthought; it happens at the start of a project when necessary

- Delivery groups have aligned around the customer.
- In the most recent re-org, for certain positions, people had the opportunity to apply for new positions.
- EX-QMO folks still get pull from various parts of the organization to facilitate Lego Serious Play exercises, retrospectives and more.
- The hierarchy grew at one point as a result of different leadership and then shrunk back as a result of new leadership.
- There's a new delivery method being co-created with an external change consultant, the newly formed change management group, and selected leaders.

CONTINUAL EVOLUTION

There's no such thing as a linear change progression of current state->transition->future state. There is only continually evolution that has ebbs and flows of energy that I'll refer to as the Waves of Change. Each wave elevates the organization to new heights and from the dawn of the organization, this is how all companies evolve.

The Commission and every other organization I've visited evolve according to this same pattern:

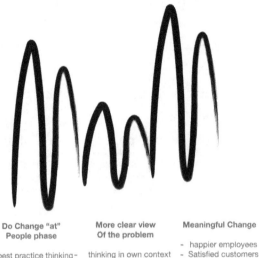

Do Change "at"   More clear view   Meaningful Change
People phase   Of the problem
                                                 - happier employees
- best practice thinking -   thinking in own context   - Satisfied customers
- Method-following   -   Fit-for-purpose change
                            approach

ASIDE: More details about *The Waves of Change* can be found at changewayfinder.com - When I wrote this book, it was only half-baked; now it's nice and toasty. You might think of the waves as maturity levels, with the difference being each wave in each organization means something different. A maturity model assumes a linear progression from state to state, regardless of context. Any given organization may go through 2 or 3 waves to reach the 2nd level of whatever maturity model they're chasing.

First Wave of Change: More superficial in nature, unclear objectives and vision, no compelling purpose, opposing systemic forces (performance mandates at odds with outcomes etc)

Things will improve, but mostly process and minor improvements, masked with marketing speak from the consultants or change team.

Example: At the commission they wanted an agile process installed. We knew *producing the wrong thing faster* wasn't helpful, but they needed to go through this wave.

Second Wave Change: Frustration that we *didn't do it right the first time* and skepticism, but more willingness to actually change things.

During the 2nd wave, there will be more clarity around the problem that needs solving and questions around why we approached the first wave the way we did. Complex change always looks more clear in retrospect.

Example: At The Commission, we moved from functional teams to cross-functional teams once the organization learned this would be more effective as opposed to making functions more agile. This wouldn't have been possible from the beginning due to the poor relationships between some functions.

Third Wave of Change: More employee and customer focus versus internal focus. While this was talked about in the first way, it was espoused theory, now it's being enacted.

Example: Spoiler alert! Digital factory, hackathons, and innovation programs started happening years after the first transformation.

The shift away from linear steps and phases, and towards managing the energy of the wave is a difficult one. Skilled change agents will develop a sixth sense in knowing when it's the right time to intervene.

They'll notice that when the wave is declining, it's a great opportunity to slow down, reflect, and revisit the purpose of the original change to inject some new life into it. While we like to plan before, and reflect after the execution phase, the reality is, you'll be progressing through multiple waves within the execution phase. Avoid the need to stay the course just because it feels icky to thing about all the time and money spent so far.

It's never too late to revisit the purpose, and remember if you're an external change agent, your part in the organizational story is limited to the first act while the employees affected by the change will have parts in all three acts.

THE INNOVATION TEAM

When we started at The Commission, we had functional Kanban boards. When the developer took a ticket to *done*, they had to go up to the 8th floor and put it in the testing team's queue. After that, work was co-ordinated at our enterprise stand up meetings. Early on in those meetings, hostility was the norm: "I'm late because YOU gave me shitty requirements!"

Eventually the organization realized that moving toward cross-functional teams was better, but they needed to go through this pain to see it.

When we created the first open space co-located working area, people freaked out. They were used to the safety of their private cube, they had plenty of desk space, dual-monitors, and plenty of storage. The first collaborative space crammed people in so tight they were practically rubbing elbows with their neighbours.

Over the span of a year, they migrated from functional teams, to cross-functional teams (Wave 1), and finally to more open collaborative team spaces (Wave N. It could have taken 7 or 8 waves of change to move from cross-functional teams to collaborative spaces. Remember, these aren't phases, these are natural evolutions that happen over a time-period that respects the organization's natural pace of change.

After those waves of change, the next evolution was to create innovation teams and they accomplished some marvellously wonderful things:

- Implemented hackathons where one app eventually went to production.
- Killed an MVP with the team members not being crucified for it because early feedback showed it wasn't the right thing to build.
- A joint business and IT team (named Digital Factory which is the new thing to copy/paste from many large organizations) implemented an application in production and won an award in the public sector.

To quickly revisit the waves of change, every organization knows that they need to innovate in some way. Every organizations knows that handing off software between departments is horribly inefficient but until the difficulty of continuing with the status quo exceeds the difficulty of the change, they won't act.

When I started at The Commission, there's no chance they would have accepted the need to create innovation teams because functional departments weren't even collaborating yet. The IT division was analogous to a manufacturing plant, hand off the widgets from function to function and check the quality at the end.

COPY, PASTE, TWEAK

Much like my bold statement that change happens waves, organizations improve when they mimic other organizations. At The Commission, the business wasn't happy with what was being delivered, and IT folks weren't engaged with the customer service division so they're understanding of the customer was limited to what the business folks were ordering.

We shifted the conversation to how they could change things, so it benefited the end-users, which was a radical difference in approaching structure and process changes.

The C-Level executives visited other organizations that were doing things they wanted to do. This is a pattern I've seen with so many organizations. They see examples of what they like from news articles, or stories on Linked In and they reach out to the leaders in those organizations to share stories. If you've worked for numerous telecoms, banks or insurance companies, you'll notice that how they work is more or less the same. It's because the same people move from company to company copying and pasting ideas, processes, and tools that they like.

It's tempting to buy operating models from big consulting firms and when I was at The Commission, that was the norm. Hire a best-of-breed consulting firm, outsource everything, or buy a best practise guide. This time they did it differently, focusing on what would benefit the end customers and engaging selected leaders from within.

THE ELUSIVE CULTURE CHANGE

When people say you can't transform unless you change the culture, this, my friends, is an attempt to shift the culture. Is it a *transformed culture*? Of course not. Certain types of organizations will always have a certain type of dominant culture, but they can create pockets of counter-culture groups.

A MANIFESTO FOR AGILE CHANGE

*H*opefully by now, you've created your agile change manifesto. While you'll be able to share and compare at changeagility.org, here are some thoughts and ideas from a couple of classes in various parts of the world.

I often get asked, *"Who gets this agile change stuff right?"* Sorry to leave some people out, but it's Finland. The Finns have a knack for being awesome at just about everything.

I remember my first foray into the agile world over 10 years ago when the word agile meant something. The early adopters of agile found four simple values and 12 timeless principles that reinforced their beliefs with a call to action for how they could improve their organizations.

It's no secret that the gold rush is on to capitalize on agile marketing, agile change management, agile bathroom tissue replacement, and business agility. But I imagine it's quite confusing for people new to agile to figure out how to sift through all the noise, marketing, and fluff to understand what the hell it means.

> *"We decided to call it a manifesto since it was a call to arms and a statement of our beliefs."*
>
> *- Martin Fowler*

When I started learning about agile, there were six books, a manifesto, and the same nine people at every meetup. It was simple. Today, there are 72 frameworks, and tens of thousands of pundits claiming expertise in agile so it's no surprise that if you want to learn about what agile is, it's confusing as hell.

I've had thousands of people through my change workshop, and there's an exercise that instructs people to create an agile change manifesto that captures the spirit of the agile manifesto. The point of this chapter is to share a few examples for those that believe *the future of agile change management has nothing to do with standards, frameworks, and process models.* Sure, these things will emerge, that's the beauty of a capitalist world, but they're all missing the point.

The reason why I say that is because my change workshop generally attracts agile coaches, employees who've been tapped on the shoulder to *make a change work,* or *traditional* change practitioners who've already worked in an agile way their whole careers without realizing it, but want to fill in a few missing pieces.

As a reminder, here's the agile manifesto:

- Individuals and interactions *over* processes and tools
- Working software *over* comprehensive documentation
- Customer collaboration *over* contract negotiation
- Responding to change *over* following a plan

That is, while there is value in the items on the right, we value the items on the left more.

Now here are a few examples of how people in my workshops have adapted that towards change:

From a group in Belgium:

- Embracing Uncertainty over reducing risk
- Facilitating Insights over telling people what to do
- Overall collaboration makes complex problem solving possible
- Co-creation over hierarchical decisions
- Overall collaboration over local optimization

From a group in Finland:

- Individuals and interactions over processes and tools
- Everyday action over comprehensive documentation
- Transparency and self-management over strict coordination and micromanagement
- Responding to change over following a plan

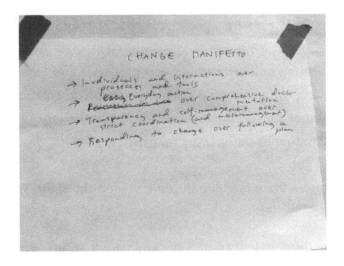

From another group in Finland:

- Understanding over techniques and tools
- Collaboration over informing
- Empowering people over managing people

From a group in Vancouver, Canada:

- Results over structures and process
- Team empowerment over hierarchy
- Regular two-way communications over proclamations
- Commitment to on-going educations/learning over one-time training

From a group in the US:

- Pull over push
- Touch over technology
- Organic over scripted
- Growth over perfection

One group even made their change manifesto out of Lego:

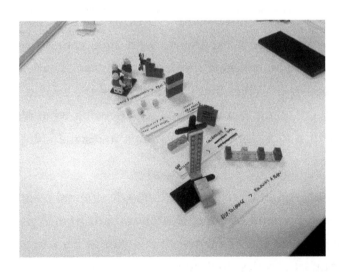

WHAT I LOVE about this exercise is that it gets people to think in their own context. We underestimate the power of personal meaning when it comes to change. We think that a set of standards and new certifications are going to help. They won't.

If you're curious, and serious enough, about wanting to learn about agile change management, don't limit yourself to what your professional association says you should learn, go explore!

Where to Learn About Agile and Change Management

My best advice for you, a change agent who is new-ish to agile, is to take a Scrum Master job in a small-ish organization. I believe it's the best way to experience true agility.

It's hard to learn agile nowadays because most of the content you'll find is related to enterprise organizations, and it's coming from people who see it as a process because that's all they know.

Odds are if your first experience with agile comes from a big organization, you're seeing the 3rd or 4th wave of agile, namely, *big-business-agile*. While that's the nature of the evolution of all ideas, you're going to miss out on experiencing what it's like to work with a kick-ass team that builds awesome solutions for customers.

Check out Agile Uprising[1] and google the take-agile-back[2] movement. A friend of mine, Ryan Lockhard from Agile Uprising, interviewed the 17 manifesto signatories back in 2016 and it's a fantastic series that revisits the intent of agile and it explores how agile has changed since 2001. You'll notice I used the word *intent* often in this book. It's important to understand why and how these ideas came to be, to internalize them, and to base your actions around them. That's not a cultist view, even though it might sound like it.

The take-agile-back movement was created by Tim Ottinger, a well-known and respected agile practitioner, back in 2014. In his view, agile became big business and process oriented. Technical excellence was put in the back seat, or in some cases left at the side of the road, and the soul was sucked out agile.

Both Agile Uprising and the take-agile-back movements are worthy of a look to help you understand that agile values the statements on the left side of the manifesto more, but does recognize that the statements on the right are still important.

There are extremists in every discipline. There are strong left-side-of-the-manifesto folks who feel personally attacked by the agile evolving into a big business and certification pyramid scheme.

On the other side, there are strong right-side-of-the-manifesto folks who only know agile as a big business because they didn't start learning about it until post-2012 when big-business-agile started emerging.

Learn from both sides, but definitely revisit the intent of the manifesto.

PART VI - CHANGE WAYFINDER

I've mentioned the Change Wayfinder many times. By the time you're reading this, it'll be full of more useful big ideas, practices and stories to inspire you to think differently about change.

I'll also reiterate that when I wrote this book in the summer of 2019, I had planned to add a bunch of short stories that you could use as inspiration.

While doing the final copyediting, I decided not to do that. Instead, I decided to put these stories, practices and ideas online at changewayfinder.com so everyone can access them without buying this book. It's part of my belief that sharing an ongoing evolution of ideas is more important than selling a book, so I broke them out into separate things. That way, you can check out the stories online without the book or buy the book and get free access to the online community. And don't worry, keep reading to find out how to get your free access, part of my than you for buying the beta version of the book!

THE CHANGE WAYFINDER WEBSITE

Before I tell you how to get free access, I wanted to share the story of the name *The Change Wayfinder*. I think you'll enjoy it.

While watching the film, *The Rise of Skywalker*, during her journey to find the emperor, Rey gets stuck. She needs help, and seeks out a wayfinder to aid her. Yeah, it's as simple as that. I though the idea of a wayfinder was great and wanted to use it in the future. that's how the name came to be.

Now, back to your free access:

Head over to changeagility.org. Enter the code: starwars and you'll get 3 months to explore the Wayfinder on the Modern Change Community.

My last decade-and-a-bit of working as a change agent has shown me that people need more on-demand help and support.

They need help creating clarity so they can move forward. Static frameworks, methods, playbook, and methods don't consider the context. A GPS, or wayfinder, knows there's a river in front of you that you probably shouldn't drive into!

Remember, change isn't a journey, it's more like continual meandering through the fog. A wayfinder can help you clear the fog to a certain degree, but the destination is always going to be changing.

HERE'S WHAT YOU'LL FIND AT THE CHANGE WAYFINDER:

For Big Thinkers: Big thinkers need big ideas that challenge their beliefs about how they see change. Start exploring modern change concepts and other big ideas and philosophies that can help you try different lenses to look at your change.

For Practical Thinkers: Pick from a variety of agile, lean startup, design thinking, and coaching and facilitation activities. All are supported with options to adapt it to your context and inspiration stories so you can see who tried them and how it worked out.

For Inspiration Seekers: Copy, paste, tweak. Humans mimic what they see and tweak it to their context. Get inspired by stories from change agents worldwide who are modernizing and contextualizing their approach to change with concrete actions.

I organized it this way for a few reasons:

- I've heard about a million times over the years, *"Yeah, sounds great in theory, but I can't do that"* - The stories on the Wayfinder provide social proof that it IS possible.
- Chefs: There are plenty of amazing change agents that just need to be poked about thinking about change differently.
- New change agents: When I was new and inexperienced, I wish I had something like this to point me to an idea or practice

- I've seen experienced and self-professed change thought-leaders get the basics of agile completely wrong because they jumped on the agile wave during the enterprise scaling and corporate me-too-ism phase. I don't mean to blame these people, but you're best to learn about *agile change* from agile coaches. Sorry. Think of this way. If you run your own business, do you want tax and accounting advice and services from someone who's been an accountant, or someone who's read a book about accounting?

Most of all, I wanted you to be able to find inspiration based on who you are and what you need. If your environment demands more structure and control, pick practices designed for that.

If you want to swing the pendulum towards co-creation, design thinking, and agile change practices, I know you'll find something.

To close off, I will end this book with a quote from my friend Don Gray. Yes, another AYE story! He ran a session called *Reading the River and* the premise was:

> "Swim with the current of the organization."

Often, as change agent, especially agile change agents, we want to disrupt. There's a time and place for swimming with the current, and a time for swimming against it.

PART VII - ACKNOWLEDGEMENTS

First and fore-most, and again, the fine folks who organized AYE and PSL which hands-down saved my life:

- Don Gray, Esther Derby, Johanna Rothman, Jerry Weinberg, and Steve Smith

I hope you know how much of a life-altering experience those events were for me.

Thanks to all of these folks, and apologies to those I forgot!

- Sue Johnston and Andrew Annett: All I do is wonder how Sue would structure a conversation, and what that one-word is that Andrew will use that makes sense of the entire universe.
- The thousands of change agents I've met over the years

from workshops and inside organizations, all of the LCM facilitators and community members who I learn from daily

- Colin Mulholland: Your breakfast story makes me smile everyday.
- Dawna Jones: Your ability think above and beyond amazes me everyday
- Julia Borgini for finding 2,943 errors in version 0.1 that I needed to merge back into Vellum!
- The Manifesto Authors: While the world feels the need to beat-up on the creators just because they're 17 white males, I still think it's timeless and inspiring
- Cynthia Barlow: One of my coaches who helped me realize it's ok to be me.
- Jean Mclendon and Hugh Gratz: For the wonderful Satir experience. Man, I have a lot of work to do.
- Doc Norton: We've met a bunch of times, but you are a great person and I am inspired by you
- Jon Stahl: We haven't worked together for a while, but you were a huge influence on how I see agile
- All of the folks I thanked in Lean Change Management!
- Jurgen Appelo: Your creativity has always been an inspiration to me
- Trevor Owens: For that first Lean Startup Machine experience that made me wonder how to use lean start-up in change
- George Carlin, plus a bunch of other standup comedians (including the ones we're not allowed to talk about anymore) - you were a wizard with words that make people think.

- This is a list of people I've met over the years that inspire me with their passion for making the world a better place (in no particular order) Esther Lind, Tabatha Cooper, Eva-Lotta Nordling, Line Degner, Andrew Guy, Adriana Girdler, April Jefferson, Aaron Dignan, Mark Raheja, Gitte Klitgaard, Mike Edwards, Dave Dame, Shahin Sheidaei, Mark O'Donovan, Barb Heller, Maria Racho.
- Most of all, to my wife and family who save my life everyday.

Oh, and if I forgot you, again, I'm sorry! Couldn't get more Canadian than that I suppose.

NOTES

1. CHASING CARS (WHY THIS BOOK? WHY NOW?)

1. https://geraldmweinberg.com/
2. http://changewayfinder.com
3. https://en.wikipedia.org/wiki/Finite_and_Infinite_Games
4. https://simonsinek.com/product/the-infinite-game/

3. HOW TO READ THIS BOOK

1. https://www.estherderby.com/
2. https://en.wikipedia.org/wiki/Open_Space_Technology
3. https://thenewkingmakers.com/
4. https://en.wikipedia.org/wiki/Imprinting_(psychology)
5. Baby Duck Syndrome - https://en.wikipedia.org/wiki/Imprinting_(psychology)#Baby_duck_syndrome
6. https://modernchangemanagement.com/change-wayfinder/

4. BEING AGILE OR DOING AGILE?

1. https://www.agilecoachinginstitute.com/
2. What is Extreme Programming - https://ronjeffries.com/xprog/what-is-extreme-programming/
3. Kerth's Prime Directive https://retrospectivewiki.org/index.php?title=The_Prime_Directive

5. BECOMING MORE FULLY HUMAN

1. The Organized Mind - https://www.penguinrandomhouse.com/books/313653/the-organized-mind-by-daniel-j-levitin/
2. Based on the work of Virginia Satir, I'll point you to Jean McLendon - https://www.satirsystems.com/JeanMcLendon.en.html (or satir-global.org)

PART I - MODERN CHANGE MANAGEMENT MANIFESTO

1. Scrum in 10 minutes by Lyssa Adkins https://www.youtube.com/watch?v=_BWbaZs1M_8
2. "The Hole-in-the-Floor Model"
   Excerpt From: Gerald M. Weinberg. "Becoming a Change Artist." (Page 20 eBook)
3. "Diffusion approach to change"
   Excerpt From: Gerald M. Weinberg. "Becoming a Change Artist." (Page 18 eBook)
4. Change is like adding milk to coffee - Niels Pflaeging https://www.linkedin.com/pulse/change-more-like-adding-milk-coffee-niels-pflaeging/
5. http://changeagility.org

1. YOUR CHANGE MANIFESTO

1. http://changeagility.org

2. INDIVIDUALS AND INTERACTIONS

1. That is, while there is value in the items on the right, we value the items on the left more. - www.agilemanifesto.org

5. RESPONDING TO CHANGE

1. https://www.darwinproject.ac.uk/people/about-darwin/six-things-darwin-never-said/evolution-misquotation
2. https://www.kodak.com/en/consumer/home

7. TOUCH OVER TECHNOLOGY

1. Julia Borgini is a long-time friend and copyeditor of my first book, I hope she wasn't mad at me! But of course, since you're reading Beta 0.2, you'll know she copyedited this version!
2. http://leandog.com

8. ADAPTABLE METRICS

1. Is the 70% Failure 'Stat' a myth? http://www.agilecoach.ca/2013/08/23/70-failure-rate-myth/

9. ADAPTING TO THE PACE

1. Otto Scharmer - Theory U https://www.ottoscharmer.com/theoryu
2. Lean Change Management - http://leanchange.management, Jason Little, 2013

12. THE PEOPLE WHO WRITE THE PLAN, DON'T FIGHT THE PLAN

1. Meaningful Change at National Leasing - https://leanchange.org/2016/11/how-to-make-change-matter-using-change-canvases/
2. Lean Change Management - Change Canvases http://leanchange.org/canvases

4. CROSS-FUNCTIONAL COLLABORATION

1. Managing Your Project Portfolio - Johanna Rothman https://www.jrothman.com/books/manage-your-project-portfolio-increase-your-capacity-and-finish-more-projects/
2. changewayfinder.com has instructions for doing this

5. INTRINSIC MOTIVATION

1. Table Group - Getting Naked by Patrick Lencioni https://www.tablegroup.com/books/getting-naked/
2. Celebration Grid by Jurgen Appelo https://management30.com/practice/celebration-grids/#:~:text=Celebration%20-Grids%20are%20a%20visual,learn%20something%20from%20our%20failures.
3. https://leanchange.org/2017/01/combining-innovation-games-and-lean-change-management/
4. From Stone Age to Agile - Ardita Karaj and Jason Little http://fromstoneagetoagile.com/

11. THE PEOPLE WHO WRITE THE PLAN DON'T FIGHT THE PLAN

1. I'm Part of an Inspiring Future https://leanchange.org/2016/07/creating-alignment-for-enterprise-transformation/
2. Open Space Technology - https://en.wikipedia.org/wiki/Open_Space_Technology
3. Lean Coffee - http://leanchange.org/leancoffee

12. INSPECT AND ADAPT

1. Lean Change Management Strategy Canvas - https://leanchange.org/resources/canvases/
2. 5 Big Takeaways from LSM Toronto - http://www.agilecoach.ca/2012/01/31/4-big-takeaways-from-lean-startup-machine-toronto/

1. TRANSFORMING HOW YOU MANAGE CHANGE WORK

1. https://retromat.org/en/?id=84-98-26-61-92
2. https://www.estherderby.com/books/

2. TRANSFORMING HOW YOU THINK ABOUT CHANGE

1. http://modernchangemanagement.com

PART V - WHAT'S CHANGE SINCE LEAN CHANGE MANAGEMENT?

1. http://leadership.mit.edu/rare-find-alan-mulally-complete-leader/

2. A MANIFESTO FOR AGILE CHANGE

1. http://agileuprising.com
2. https://www.infoq.com/articles/taking-back-agile/

Printed in the USA
CPSIA information can be obtained
at www.ICGtesting.com
LVHW010146290723
753587LV00027B/246